BALDWIN COUNTY GEORGIA LOTTERY DRAWERS
for 1820 and 1821

By
Michael A. Ports

Copyright © 2016
Michael A. Ports
All Rights Reserved

Printed for Clearfield Company by
Genealogical Publishing Company
Baltimore, Maryland
2016

ISBN 978-0-8063-5812-3

Made in the United States of America

Table of Contents

Table of Contents	1
Introduction	2
Baldwin County Militia Districts	4
1820 Land Lottery	6
Dozier's, Ellis', Haws', Norris', and Russell's Districts	10
State Copy of Marshall's and Taliaferro's Districts	33
County Copy of Marshall's and Taliaferro's Districts	58
Irwin's and Stephen's Districts	81
Fortunate Drawers	94
1821 Land Lottery	122
Major Amos Young's Battalion	125
Major R. W. Ellis' Battalion	145
Index	203

Introduction

The Georgia Department of Archives and History has three rolls of microfilm of various Land Lottery records held by the Baldwin County Court of Ordinary. The first roll, filmed by the Georgia Archives in 1967 and located in Drawer 187, Roll 74, is titled

BALDWIN COUNTY – 1820 Lottery, Those Entitled to Draw from Nine Districts and Prize Winners.

The first roll contains a photocopy of the law authorizing the Third Land Lottery, also known as the 1820 Land Lottery, and three lists of participants. The first is a list of residents entitled to draw from five of the nine militia districts comprising the county, referred to as the County Copy as the original is in the possession of the County. The second is a list of the residents entitled to draw from the remaining four militia districts, referred to as the State Copy as the original is among the records of the Surveyor General's Department at the Georgia Department of Archives and History. The third, titled Baldwin 1820 on the microfilm, is a list of Baldwin County residents who won prizes in the lottery and referred to as Fortunate Drawers. Taken together, the three provide a complete list of those Baldwin County residents entitled to draw as well as the prize winners of the 1820 Land Lottery. Following the three lists is a series of typewritten tables identifying the nine militia districts and their captains for the six years from 1817 through 1822, prepared from the tax digests by Mr. Frank Hudson. Those tables appear immediately following the Introduction.

The second microfilm roll, filmed by the Genealogical Society of Salt Lake City, Utah in 1965, is located in Drawer 139, Roll 71. The original volume, titled *Land Lottery 1821, Baldwin County*, appears to consist of three separate books rebound into one volume. Bound in the back of the book, apparently in error, are two lists for Taliaferro's and Marshall's Districts for the 1820 Lottery. The two lists, referred to as the County Copies, are nearly identical to those in the State Copy kept by the Surveyor General's Department.

The third microfilm roll, filmed by the Georgia Archives in 1969, is titled

Baldwin County Ordinary
1820 Land Lottery

Alphabetical listing of those entitled to draw.

The roll appears to be a subsequent filming of the State Copy for the districts commanded by Captains Marshall and Taliaferro.

For the most part, the handwriting of the various clerks is legible, making the transcription straightforward and not too difficult. The occasional ink smear, damaged paper, torn page, or other imperfection is noted in brackets, for example [smudge]. Sometimes, the small letters "a" and "o" appear indistinguishable, making abbreviations such as Jas. and Jos. impossible to distinguish. Their formation of the letters "n" and "r" at the end of surnames can be problematic to decipher. Also, the various clerks formed the capital letters "I" and "J" identically. Determining which letter usually is straightforward when the first letter of a name, but entirely a guess when an initial. The transcription follows Sperry's recommended guidelines for reading early script.[1] The transcription does not correct any grammar or spelling, no matter how obvious the errors, but does add a few commas for clarity. Following the transcriptions, the index includes the full names of all the persons mentioned.

The book is dedicated to the memory of Abel and Charlotte (Harrell) Hodges, early settlers of Baldwin County and two members of the Georgia branch of the author's family tree. Many thanks are offered to the very knowledgeable staff at the Georgia Department of Archives and History for their patience and assistance not in just locating the subject records, but in understanding the context of the records. Thanks also are offered Joe Garonzik of the Genealogical Publishing Company for his professional advice and counsel. Special thanks are due Marcia Tremonti for her patience and encouragement through this challenging, but interesting endeavor.

---

[1] Sperry, Kip, *Reading Early American Handwriting*. Genealogical Publishing Company, Inc., Baltimore, Maryland, Sixth Printing, 2008.

Baldwin County Militia Districts

While the Georgia Militia today is extinct, in the sense that it existed during the Revolutionary War, the War of 1812, the several Indian uprisings, and the Civil War, Georgia Militial Districts remained relevant to the lives of everyday Georgians throughout the nineteenth and much of the twentieth centuries, affecting the jurisdiction of the Justice of the Peace Courts, property tax returns, land conveyance in headright counties, election district boundaries, and stock and fence laws. In 1784, after the close of the Revolutionary War, the legislature significantly amended the militia law, requiring the captain of every district to enroll the names of all men between the ages of 16 and 50 into their militia company. Although the various militia districts were numbered, through most of the first half of the nineteenth century, the districts usually were identified by the name of the commanding captain. The table below identifies the names of the captains for each militia district for the years 1817 through 1822. The following map shows the militia district boundaries as they existed in 1952.

District	1817	1818	1819
321	Irwin's	Irwin's	Irwin's
322	Stephens'	Stephens'	Stephens'
319	Ellis'	Ellis'	Ellis'
	Haws'	Haws'	Haws'
318	Woodward's	Cousins'	Norris'
320	Milledgeville	Milledgeville	Milledgeville
105	Hightower's	Hightower's	Russell's
115	Buchanan's	Buchanan's	Taliaferro's
317	Wiggins'	Wiggins'	Dozier's

District	1820	1821	1822
321	McCrarey's	McCrarey's	James McCrarey's
322	Stephens'	Stephens'	Lewis Stephens'
319	McGehee's	McGehee's	James McGehee's
	Haws'	Haws'	Claiburn Haws'
318	Doles'	Doles'	Benjamin Doles'
320	Milledgeville	Milledgeville	Milledgeville (Huson's)
105	Russell's	Russell's	Russell's
115	Lacey's	White's	Benjamin White's
317	Dozier's	Dozier's	Jane Dozier's
			V. E Vickers, Malcolm's

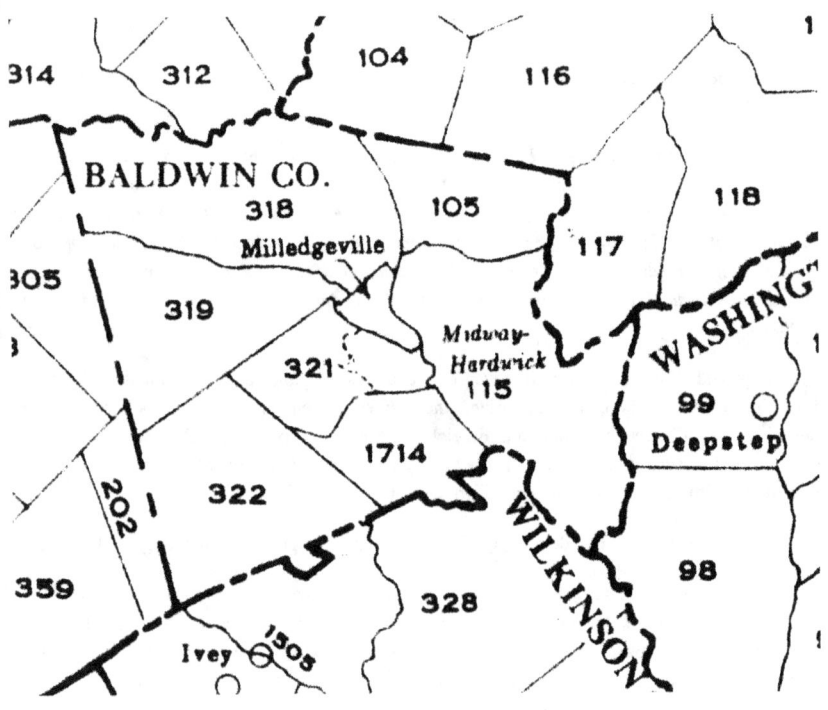

Baldwin County Militia Districts[2]

---

[2] Historic Maps, Surveyor General, RG 3-8-65, Georgia Archives.

1820 Land Lottery

On December 15, 1818, Governor William Rabun signed the law authorizing the 1820 land Lottery, titled

An Act, to dispose of and distribute the late cession of land obtained from the Creek and Cherokee nations of Indians by the United States, by the several treaties, one concluded at Fort Jackson, on the ninth day of August, in the year eighteen hundred and fourteen, and one concluded at the Cherokee Agency, on the eighth day of July, in the year of our Lord one thousand eight hundred and seventeen, and one concluded at the Creek Agency, on Flint river, the twenty-second day of January, in the year of our Lord on thousand eight hundred and eighteen.

The act provided for the creation of seven new counties, Appling, Early, Gwinnett, Habersham, Hall, Irwin, and Walton, and authorized the Surveyor General to divide each county into numbered land districts and each land district into numbered lots. After the completion of the surveys and returns made to the Surveyor General, the State printed lottery tickets, each designated with the county name, land district number, and the lot number.

The act provided specific and detailed qualifications for participation in the lottery, as follows

...every male white person of eighteen years of age and upwards, being a citizen of the United States, and an inhabitant of this state three years immediately preceding the passage of this act, including such as have been absent on lawful business, and all who served as drafted men or volunteers in the late Indian war, whose residence has not been three years in this state, and are now citizens of this state; Provided, they have resided, and continue to reside in this state since the time of said service or services being performed, shall be entitled to one draw; that all officers and soldiers of the revolutionary war, who are indigent or invalid, and who were engaged and fought as such, on behalf of the United States, in said revolutionary war, shall be and they are hereby authorized to have two draws in addition to those heretofore authorized by law; and should any such officer or soldier aforesaid have been a fortunate drawer in either of the land lotteries heretofore drawn in this state, he shall be, and he is hereby entitled to one draw in this lottery, and shall be excepted from the general provisions of the oath prescribed by this act, so far as regards that part of said oath which requires persons to swear that they have not been fortunate drawers in either of the previous lotteries in this state; Provided, the said officer or soldier shall swear that he is indigent or invalid, and that he was, as such officer or soldier, engaged in the service of, and fought in behalf of the United States in said revolutionary war; and that all widows or orphans, whose husbands or fathers were killed in the late wars with Great Britain and the Indians, shall be entitled to one draw, in addition to those already allowed by this act to widows and orphans; every male persons of like description, having a wife or legitimate male child or children, under the age of eighteen years, or unmarried female child or children, shall be entitled to two draws; all widows, with like residence, shall be entitled to one

draw; all families of orphans resident as aforesaid, under the age of twenty-one years, except such as may be entitled in their own right to draw of draws, whose father is dead, shall be entitled to one draw; and all families of orphans, consisting of more than two, having neither father nor mother living, shall have two draws; but if not exceeding two, then such orphan or orphans shall be entitled to one draw, which shall be given in the county and district where the eldest of said orphan or orphans, or guardian resides; Provided nevertheless, that the person or persons that drew a prize or prizes in the late land lotteries, shall be excepted from any participation in the present lottery, except families of orphans consisting of more than one persons, and such other persons as are herein excepted; Provided also, that the citizens of this state, who come under the provisions of this act as above contemplated, and who were legally drafted in the late war against Great Britain or the Indians, and refused to serve a tour of duty, either in person or by a substitute, shall not be entitled to the provisions of this act, as above contemplated; nor any of those who evaded a draft by leaving the state or county in which they resided, for that purpose. And if any minor or minors should draw land, the guardian of said minor or minors shall have the right or privilege of applying to the Governor, and obtain the grant or grants therefor, upon the payment of lawful fees; but said guardian shall not be permitted to sell said land during the minority of said minor or minors.

The legislation directed the county inferior courts to appoint persons in each district to compile lists of persons entitled to draw, within three months from the passage of the act, the lists to be entered into a book by militia district, giving the names of persons and the number of draws to which they were entitled in alphabetical order. One copy of the book was to be deposited in the office of the clerk of the Superior Clerk and the other sent to the state. Contrary to the terms of the legislation, in practice, the Inferior Courts in most, if not all, counties took possession of the records. The act required each person to take an oath substantiating their eligibility and pay 25 cents per draw before their name could be entered.

The act further directed the Governor to print blank lottery tickets, equal in number to the whole number of draws and enter the names of each person, with the name of the county, militia district, and other identifying remarks, and deposit the tickets in one wheel. A second wheel was filled with the tickets printed with designated land lots and sufficient blank tickets so that the two wheels contained the same number of tickets. Then after giving one months' notice, the lottery began by drawing one ticket from each wheel as nearly simultaneously as possible and delivering them to the managers of the drawing, who recorded the winning names in a book with the lot number, land district number, and county.

And, finally, the act further provided

That all persons against whose names lands may be drawn in pursuance of this act, shall be entitled to receive grants for the same, vesting in them fee simple titles, on paying into the treasury of this state the sum of eighteen dollars for each tract so drawn and granted, in lieu of all fees of office and other charges for surveying and granting the said lands; Provided nevertheless, That if any person or persons, entitled to such grant or grants, shall fail to pay the aforesaid sum, and take out such grant or grants within two years from the completion of the lottery, except as hereinbefore excepted, the same shall revert to and be vested in this state.

On December 16, 1819, Governor John Clark signed legislation amending the Act of 1818. The amendments modified some county boundaries, a few land district designations, the rules governing surveyors and those appointed to register the eligible drawers, and other administrative procedures.

The following table summarizes the land districts and lot sizes for each of the new counties.

County	Land Districts	Lot Sizes
Appling	Districts 1-13	490 acres
Early	Districts 1-23 and 26-28	250 acres
Gwinnett	Districts 5-7	250 acres
Habersham	Districts 1-4 and 10-13	250 acres
Habersham	Districts 5-6	490 acres
Hall	Districts 8-12	250 acres
Irwin	Districts 1-16	490 acres
Rabun	Districts 1 and 3-5	490 acres
Rabun	District 2	250 acres
Walton	Districts 1-4	250 acres

The grant for each lot cost $18, regardless of the size of the lot.

On June 11 and 18, 1820, the following notice appeared in the *Georgia Journal*, published at Milledgeville.

> *Executive Department, Georgia*
> *Milledgeville, 8th June, 1820*
> *The Commissioners of the Land Lottery being convened at this place for the purpose of making the necessary preparations for the same, having*

> informed the Executive that they will be in readiness to proceed to the drawing of said Lottery on the 18th of August next.
>
> Notice is therefore given in pursuance of the 16th section of the law of the General Assembly of this State, dated 15th December, 1818, that the drawing of the said Lottery will commence at the State-House on Friday the 18th day of the ensuing month.
>
> By order of the Governor,
>
> William F. Steele, Secretary
>
> The editors of the Georgian, at Savannah, the Augusta Chronicle, and the News at Washington, will give the above two insertions in their respective papers.

On August 15, 22, and 29, 1820, an additional notice appeared in the Georgia Journal.

> Executive Department, Georgia
>
> Milledgeville, 5th August, 1820
>
> The Commissioners of the Land Lottery having informed the Executive that they will not be prepared to commence drawing the same sooner than Friday the first day of September next;
>
> Notice is therefore given, in pursuance of the 16th section of the law of the General Assembly of this State, dated 15th December, 1818, that, on Friday the first day of September next, the drawing of said Land Lottery will commence at the State-House.
>
> By order of the Governor,
>
> John Burch, Secretary
>
> The editors of the Georgian, the Augusta Chronicle, and News, are requested to discontinue the notice in relation to the Land Lottery heretofore published in their papers, and insert the above.

The lottery drawing began September 1st and continued until December 2nd.

Dozier's, Ellis', Haws', Norris', and Russell's Districts

The following transcription is the first of the three lists on the first roll of microfilm and includes the residents of Baldwin County entitled to draw from the five militia districts commanded by Captains Dozier, Ellis, Haws, Norris (or Cousins), and Russell. The list consists of a table with nine columns, but the columns are not identified. On a separate sheet, apparently not bound in the original volume, a clerk wrote the following column headings.

Names of Applicants

Applicants Generally

Widows

Widows of persons who died in the public service during the late wars

Orphans of persons who died in the late wars with Britain & Indians

Orphans

Revolutionary Officers and Soldiers

Persons who Served during the late Seminole Wars

In the first column, the names of the applicants appear in approximate alphabetical order by the first letter of the last name, arranged by militia district. The next seven columns include the number of draws to which each applicant was entitled in each of the categories, followed by the total number of draws in the last, or rightmost, column.

On the first page of the original volume, a clerk wrote

Watsons Battalion District
Registered By Robert Wynn
March the 15 1819

Ellises District								
Appleby, Henrey	1							
Cousin's District								
Anderson, Gideon	1							
Allums, Whitfieald	1							
Allums, John	2							
Dozier's District								
Anders, Stephen R.	2							
Anderson, James	1							
Anders, Joseph	2							
Ellieses District								
Bivins, James	2						2	
Bivins, Shedrick	2						2	
Bivins, John	1						1	
Brown, Hollinger	2						2	
Brown, Mark	2						2	
Brown, Mathew	1						1	
Beckhannan, Green B.								
Buckhanan, Sarah		1						
& for orphans of Robert Buchanan						1		1
Barrentine, John	1						1	
Brantley, Edmund	2						2	
Barrew, Lucy			1					1
& for the orphans of James						1		1

Barrow						
Boynton, Moses	2					2
Baker, Jeremiah	2					
Baker, Jane		1				1
& for the orphards of Julius Wickers				1		1
Beal, Tanday	2					2
Cozins' District						
Brown, Stephen A.	1					1
Beasly, William	2					2
Beasley, John J.	1					1
Butts, Lewis	1					1
Braser, Henrey	2					2
Babb, Elizabeth		1				1
Bass, Martha		1				1
Russel's District						
Brown, William	1					1
Byington, Amos F.	2					2
Bodnax, Elizabeth R.		1				1
Blakey, David	2					2
Bass, Sterling	2					2
Dozier's District						
Barrentine, Jacob	2					2
Brooks, Samuel	2					2
Burnside, James	2					2

Barksdell, Terrell	2						2
& for the orphans of John Brksdell					1		1
Hawses District							
Burt, Robert	2						2
Bridges, Reuben	1						1
Bridges, James	1						1
Barnard, John	2						2
Ellis District							
Cooper, Thomas	2						2
Cooper, Davis	2						2
Collins, Moses	1						1
Collins, Aaron	1						1
Collins, Robert	2					2	4
Cavenah, George	2						2
Callaway, Elijah	2						2
Callaway, Levin	2						2
Callaway, Elisha	1						1
Cook, Henry	1						1
Cook, Arthur B.	1						1
Colman, William	1						1
Colman, Sarah		1					1
& for the orphans of Thomas Colman					1		1
Curry, Cary	2					2	4

Curry, Elisha	1							1
Chapman, Ambroes for the orphans of Laban Chapman					1			1
Colman, Willis	2							2
Cozins's District								
Clower, Thomas	2							2
Cone, James	2							2
Collins, James	2							2
Cousins, Green & for the	2							2
Orphan of Christopher Rutledge					1			1
Cunningham, Samuel	2							2
Crittenden, Robert G.	2							2
Collins, Joseph	2							2
Clark, John	1							1
Clements, Stephen	2							2
Russel's District								
Clarke, Alfred	2							2
Currie, John H.	1							1
Currie, Sarah		1						1
& for John C. Currie orphans					1			1
Callaway, Sarah		1						1
Cobb, Levi	2							2
Dozier's District								
Clem, Henrey	2							2

Calhoon, Phillip	2							2
& for the orphan of Michael Calhoon					1			1
Cook, William	2							2
Calhoon, Elbert	2							2
Hawses Ditrict								
Cone, John	2					2		4
Clements, Thomas	2							2
Cochram, Thomas	2							2
Cone, Joseph	1							1
Cone, Brazzel	2							2
Ellis[es] District								
Dismuck, Betsy &		1						1
for the orphins of John Dismucks					1			1
Dunivent, Daniel &	2							2
for Fountain Dawson					1			1
Davis, Thomas	2							2
Daniel, William	1							1
Daniel, Young	1							1
Davice, Esaw	1							1
Davice, William	2							2
Captain Coussins'								
Dorsey, Jackey B & L		1						1
For Denis Dorsey's orphans					1			1

Doles, Jesse & for the	2				2		4
Orphans of Lemon Doles				1			1
Doles, Benjamin	2						2
Densler, Henry	2						2
Russels' District							
Danely, Arthur	1						1
Dozier's District							
Dozier, Agness		1					1
Dozier, James P. &	2						2
for the orphans of Abram Settle				1			1
Downer, John	2						2
Haws District							
Davice, Hugh					1		1
Darbey, James	2						2
Ellis' District							
Ellis, Richard W.	2						2
Ellis, Thomas M.	1						1
Edwards, William	2						2
Ellis, Fielding	2						2
Ellis, Austin	1						1
Ellis, William	2						2
Dozier's District							
Evans, Turner	2						2
Evans, Elizabeth &		1					1

for the orphans of John Evans					1		1
Haws District							
Evans, Thomas	2						2
Ellis District							
Fields, Thompson	2						2
Cozins District							
Flewellen, Ann &		1					1
for the orphan of Abner Flewellen, viz Margaret Flewellen					1		1
Fuller, Jones	2						2
Russel's District							
Freeney, Elijah	1						1
Dozier's District							
Ford, Francis	2						2
Haws' District							
Flake, John P.	1						1
Ellis' District							
Grant, Priscilla		1					1
& for the orphans of Joseph Grant					1		1
Cousins' District							
Gill, William	1						1
Gill, Jesse	1						1
Gault, John Henry	1						1

Ruzzel's District									
Griggs, John							1		1
Godwin, William F.	1								1
Godwin, James	2								2
Dozier's District									
Green, Raligh	1								1
Greene, Myles	2								2
Goslin, Barnet	1								1
Green, John H.	2								2
Goslin, James	1								1
Gardner, Elias	1								1
Haws' District									
Gachet, Benjamin	2								2
Ellis' District									
Hawkins, William	2								2
Harp, Dixon	2								2
Hodnett, William	1								1
Hill, Robert H.	2								2
Hill, James A.	1								1
Horn, William	1								1
Horn, James	2								2
Cousins' District									
Harvey, William &	2								2
for Rachel Harvey orphan					1				1

Humpres, James C.	2							2
Humphres, Thomas J.	1					2		3
Huff, Edward	2							2
Harvey, Micael	1							1
Huff, Travace	1							1
Harvey, Rebecca		1						1
Huff, William H.	1							1
Holt, Sarah		1						1
Harvey, Stephen	1							1
Russel's District								
Hightower, Pleasant R.	2							2
Hubbard, John	1							1
Hubbard, Manoah	2					2		4
Hill, Judeath &		1						1
for orphans of Tho[s] Hill					1			1
Dozier's District								
Howel, William	2							2
Holt, Alfred B.	1							1
Hines, Abner	2							2
Hawz[s] District								
Hendrick, Gustavus	2							2
& for the orphans of John Hendrick					2			2
Haws, Clabourn	2							2
Haws, Newton	2							2

Horton, Edmund & for	2							2
orphans of Robert Freeney					1			1
Hogan, Isham & for	2							2
orphans of Marshal Smith					1			1
The or the orphans of Bartlett Ham					1			1
Harris, Ezekiel	2							2
Ellis' District								
Jones, L. Henry	2							2
Jolly, John	2							2
Jolly, Asa	1							1
Jolly, James	2							2
Cousins District								
Jackson, Susannah		1						1
Johnson, Samuel	2							2
Jackson, Sarah		1						1
Russels District								
Jeane, Greene	2							2
Dozier's District								
Jackson, Jacob	2							2
Johnston, Gideon	2							2
Jackson, Thomas	1							1
Johnston, Loid	1							1
Johnston, William	2							2
Jones, John W.	2							2

Haws' District								
Jones, John A.	2							2
Jenkins, Benjamin	2							2
Cousins' District								
King, John & for	2							2
orphan of James Jackson Irby					1			1
Dozier's District								
Kemp, Simeon &	2							2
for the orphans of Stephen Horton					1			1
Haws' District								
Kilpatrick, Richard	2							2
& for orphans of Bretian Ganday					1			1
Ellis' District								
Lacy, Philemon	2							2
Long, Nancy & for		1						1
Drury Long's orphans				1				1
Leonard, Francis	1							1
Lawson, John H. & for	2							2
orphans of Samuel Dent				1				1
Leonard, James C.	1							1
Russel's District								
Lafield, John	2							2
Dozier's District								

Little, Allen & for	1							1
the orphans of Drury Womble					1			1
Lester, William C.	1							1
Lester, James, S						1		1
Haws' District								
Lester, Hiram	2							2
Lester, Isaac, Sen[r]	2							2
Lester, John	1							1
Lester, Isaac, Jun[r]	1							1
Lester, Wade	1							1
Ledbetter, Henry	1							1
Ledbetter, William	1							1
Low, Edmund	2							2
Ledbetter, Sarah		1						1
Ellis' District								
McGinty, Meashack	2							2
Marcus, Mary		1						1
Miles, John	2							2
Miles, Robert P.	1							1
McGehee, James & for	2							2
orphans of Edward McGehee					1			1
Miles, Thomas	2							2
McCrary, Robert	2							2

McKinney, Jane & for		1						1
the orphans of William McKiney					1			1
McKinney, William	1							1
McKinney, John	1							1
Martin, John L.	2							2
Moran, James	1							1
Cousins' District								
McDonald, Archibald	1							1
Mecham, Henry, S^{nr}	2							2
Meeks, Britton & for						2		2
the orphans of Edmund Cooper					1			1
Mathews, Josiah & for	2							2
The orphan Joseph Brown					1			1
Mathews, Abraham	2							2
Mallet, James	2							2
Mallet, Randol	1							1
Moore, Morrace for the orphan of James Smith					1			1
Myrick, John & for	2							2
John Little'z orphans					2			2
Meacham, Henry, J^{r}	1							1
Myrick, James	2							2
Mercer, Francis	2							2
Moore, Luke							1	1

Murphy, James H.	1						1
McMulling, James	1						1
Russel's District							
Moore, Whittington	1						1
Moore, Levinah		1					1
Moore, John, S^{nr}	1						1
Miller, Jacob	2						2
Marchman, John	2						2
Moore, John, Ju^{nr}	2						2
McGinty, Abednego	1						1
McGinty, Robert	2						2
Mitchel, D. B. S^{enr}	2						2
Mitchel, Wm Stephens	1						1
Dozier's District							
Moughon, Thomas	2						2
McClowd, Hugh	2						2
Haws' District							
Moreland, Elisha	1						1
Martin, Benjamin	2						2
Mims, Williamson	2						2
Myrick, Goodwin	2						2
& for the orphans of Stebb Parham					1		1
Methvin, Nathard	2					-	2
Moore, Clement	2						2

Methvin, Benjamin	1						1
Methvin, Joseph	1						1
Moore, Spencer	2						2
Moore, Elijah	2						2
Morris, Joseph	1						1
Morris, Joseph	1						1
Morris, James	2						2
Ellis' District							
Owen, Aaron	2						2
Hawz' District							
Oates, James	2						2
Ellis' District							
Parker, Polley & for		1					1
Jacob Parker's orphins					1		1
Parsons, Josiah	2						2
Pool, Laban	1						1
Parker, Sarah		1					1
Cousins' District							
Palmore, Christopher	1						1
Parham, Boreland	2						2
Parker, George	2						2
Russel's District							
Preston, David	2						2
Petts, Noel	1						1

Petts, John	2					2
Petts, Jack	1					1
Dozier's District						
Pearman, Oranj	2					2
Haws' District						
Peters, Sarah & for		1				1
John Peters' orphans				1		1
Picket, Elizabeth		1				1
Picket, Betsey & for		1				1
William Picket's orphans				1		1
Parham, Thomas S.	2					2
Pumphrey, Reason	1					1
Peters, Robinson	2					2
Patton, William D.	1					1
Perdue, James A.	2					2
& for orphan of John Wood				1		1
Perdue, John D.	2					2
Perdue, George	2					2
Peters, William	1					1
Russel's District						
Quinn, William	2					2
Ellis' District						
Redding, John	2					2
Redding, Parham	1					1

Rice, Nancy & for		1						1
John Rice orphans					1			1
Rice, James	2							2
Richirson, Elbert	1							1
Rogers, George W.	2							2
Reed, Zephiniah	2							2
Reynolds, Sarah & for		1						1
the orphan of Joshua Reynolds					1			1
Reid, Jane		1						1
Reid, Jeremiah	1							1
Cousins' District								
Redding, Ezekiel	2							2
Russels District								
Russel, Martin, C	2							
Russel, John	1							
Ryan, Risden	1							
Russel, James							1	
Dozier's District								
Redding, Edith		1						
Runnels, William	2							
Rew, James & for	2							
John Hammet orphan					1			1
Redding, Thomas	2							
Robertson, Henry	2							

Redding, James D.	2						
Haws' District							
Runnels, Robert	2						2
Runnels, James	2						2
Ellis' District							
Sharp, Cyrus	1						1
Scurlock, Joshua						1	1
Simons, John, S^{nr}					1		1
Cousins' District							
Sims, Benjamin	2						2
Smith, Samuel T.	1						1
Shepperd, David &	1						1
for the orphans of Chas Shepperd					1		1
Scoggin, James	1						1
Sale, Gideon	2						2
Stephens, William	1						1
Russel's District							
Skinner, Flora &		1					1
for orphans of Henry Skinner					1		1
Scott, Ross	1						1
Scott, John R.	2						2
Sims, Bartlet	1						1
Dozier's District							

Searcy, William	2							2
& for orphans of Aaron Searcy					1			1
Searcy, Aaron	2							2
Simpson, William	2							2
Sims, Judith		1						1
Snipes, William B.	1							1
Smallpiece, Ann		1						1
& for orphan of Thomas P. Smallpiece					1			1
Haws' District								
Stevens, John	2							2
Sheppard, Thomas	1							1
Sheppard, William	2							2
Smith, John							2	2
Ellis' District								
~~Talbot, Benjamin~~	~~2~~						~~2~~	4
Cousins' District								
Tomlinson, James	1							1
Tomlinson, Mary &		1						1
for the orphans of John Tomlinson					1			1
Tarentine, Samuel	1							1
Taylor, Bartholomew	2							2
Talbot, Benjamin	2						2	4
Russel's District								

Turner, Wilson	1						1
Thomas, James	2						2
Dozier's District							
Thompson, Henry	2						2
Haws' District							
Thomas, Spencer, Sen[r]	2						2
Thomas, Spencer, Jun[r]	1						1
Thomas, Gracy & for		1					1
the orphans of Jonathan Thomas				1			1
Tinsley, Samuel						1	1
Ellis' District							
Varner, Alexandria	2						2
Vincent, Benjamin	2				—		2
Haws' District							
Veazey, James	1						1
Veazey, Thomas	2						2
Ellis' District							
Waller, Elizabeth		1					1
Worsham, George S.	1						1
Winaham, John	2						2
Works, Eli	1						1
Walker, Eli	2						2
Cousins' District							
White, Benadick	2						2

Watson, Alexander	1						1
Wittingham, Charles M.	2						2
Watson, Samuel	1						1
Watson, Robert	1						1
Wheler, Asberry	2						2
Watson, John, Se^n	2						2
Wheler, Jesse	2						2
Wheler, Henry	1						1
Waltern, Henry W.	1						1
Watson, James C. &	2						2
for the orphan of Andrew Collins					1		1
also for the orphans of Isaac Barnett, viz Je^{my} & Jno					1		1
Watson, John	1						1
Willingham, James	1						1
Watson, William C.	2						2
Womack, Green	1						1
Russel's District							
Wright, Abednigo, Senr	2						2
Woodbrooks, William	2						2
Dozier's District							
Winn, Baylor	2						2
Warren, Robert	2						2
Woodall, Jacob	2						2

Womack, Mark	1							1
Watson, John						1		1
Haws' District								
Williams, William	2							2
Williams, Winfrey	1							1
Walker, Baurshayba		1						1
Ellis' District								
Youngblood, Thomas	1							1
Russel's District								
Yats, Willis	1							1
Haws' District								
Young, Thomas	2							2
& for the orphans of Turner Young					1			1
Yeargam, Benjamin H.	1							1

On what appears to be the last page of the original volume, the Ordinary, M. R. Bell, recorded the mark and brand of Wednesday Butts on December 19, 1870.

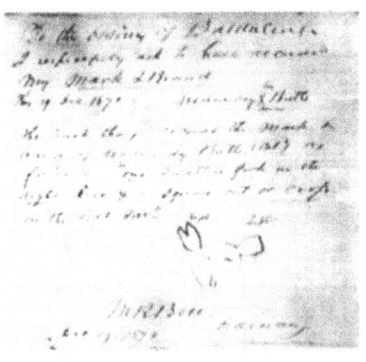

State Copy of Marshall's and Taliaferro's Districts

The following transcription is from the second list on the first microfilm roll, referred to as the State Copy, which includes the residents of Baldwin County entitled to draw from the four militia districts commanded by Captains Irwin, Marshall, Stephens, and Taliaferro. From the microfilm, the State Copy appears to consist of two separate original volumes. The first volume includes the lists from two militia districts, with Captain Marshall's District appearing on the left hand pages and Captain Taliaferro's District appearing on the right hand pages. In a similar manner, the second volume includes two districts, with Captain Stephens' District appearing on the left hand pages and Captain Irwin's District appearing on the right hand pages. Again, the lists are in a columnar format, but the columns are not identified, but appear to be the same as the headings for the County Copy.

As noted in the Introduction, both the County Copy and the State Copy of the two lists of eligible drawers for Taliaferro's and Marshall's District survive. The two copies nearly are identical, but have the following differences.

Marshall's, or Milledgeville, District:

1. Nathan Brady, Junr is spelled Braddy on the State Copy

2. William J. Dannelly is pelled Daniel on the State Copy.

3. Amasa Doud is spelled Daud on the State Copy

4. On the County Copy, following the entry for Amasa Daud, is the entry for Dunnivant, Abel, which does not appear on the State Copy.

5. Rhodam A. Green is spelled Rodham on the State Copy.

6. On the County Copy, following the entry for Hardy P. Humphrey, are the entries for Edy Howard and John Howard, which do not appear on the State Copy.

7. On the County Copy, the entry for Overoff Jordan has 2 draws in the first column and 2 draws in the sixth column, making a total of 4 draws instead of 2, but on the State Copy he only has 2 draws.

8. On the County Copy, Hezekiah Jordan is noted as "by his Father Overoff Jordan," but on the State Copy he is noted as 'by O. Jordan."

9. On the County Copy, Mildred S. Ketler has a middle initial, but the State Copy she doed not.
10. On the County Copy, following the entry for Philip Logan, is the entry for Joel Logan, which doed not appear on the State Copy.
11. On the County Copy, the entry reads, "Locke, Abner, Guardian for Elizabeth and Obedience Lowe, orphans of O. Lowe, dec^d," but on the State Copy reads, "Locke, Abner, Guardian for Elizabeth and Obedience Lowe."
12. On the County Copy, the entry reads, Locke, Abner, Guardian for Washington Dawson, orphan of John Dawson," but on the State Copy reads, "Locke, Abner, Guardian for Washington Dawson."
13. On the County Copy, the entry reads, "Locke, Mary, for Jesse Locke, orphan of Jonathan Locke," but on the State Copy reads, "Locke, Mary for orphan of Jonathan Locke."
14. The entry for Lamar, C. Q. Lucius appears of the State Copy, but not on the County Copy.
15. On the State Copy, the entry appears as Miles, Meadows, but on the County Copy as Meadows, Miles.
16. The entry on the State Copy is spelled Chancey Rowe, but on the County Copy is spelled Chauncey Rowe.
17. The entry on the State Copy is spelled Stephen Saunders, but on the County Copy is spelled Stephen Sanders.
18. On the County Copy, the entry for John Kraatz appears in Taliaferro's District, but in Marshall's District on the State Copy.

Taliaferro's District:

1. The entry for Nathaniel Miller reads, "for the orphans of Joseph L. Slade" on the County Copy, but appears to read, "for the orphans of Joseph T. Slade" on the State Copy.

Marshall's							
Atkinson, Littleton	1						1
Allen, Harris	2						2
Allen, John	2						2
Ayers, William	1						1
Taliaferro's							
Austin, John	1						1
Akridge, John	1						1
Akridge, Abel	2						2
Allen, Cousie		1					1
Marshall's							
Blithe, J. Anne				1			1
Bird, Thompson	2						2
Bird, John C.	1						1
Bridggers, James C.	1						1
Boon, John	2						2
Betts, Elisha	2						2
Brown, John U.	2						2
Britton, Harriet		1					1
Britton, Harriet for orphans of John Britton				1			1
Boon, William	1						1
Brown, Phebe		1					1
Brown, Phebe for orphan of William Brown				1			1

Betton, Solomon	2							2
Brown, Samuel							1	1
Barron, Joseph	2							2
Buchannan, H. L. Revinus	1							1
Ball, William	2							2
Bozeman, John	2							2
Barrow, James, Sen[r]	1							1
Bevin, William	2							2
Bevin, William for orphans of Shadrack Bevin					1			1
Brown, William	2							2
Burgy, Henry	2							2
Bower, Bennannuel	1							1
Burden, Elizabeth		1						1
Baxter, Thomas W.	2							2
Barrow, Jacob	2							2
Barrow, Jacob for orphan of Moses Barrow					1			1
Betton, Charles F. M.	1							1
Braddy, Nathan, Jun[r]	1							1
Bowles, David	1							1
Bevin, William	1							1
Bradford, Thomas M.	1							1
Berry, James	1							1
Beckam, Absalon B.	1							1

Bulger, Daniel	2						2
Bush, Henry	1						1
Bowers, Arthur	2						2
Bozeman, James	2						2
Barrow, William	1						1
~~Brown, Thomas C.~~	1						1
~~Babb, William~~	2						2
Bostwick, Anne		1					1
Bostwick, Anne for orphans of Chesley Bostwick					1		1
Buffington, Samuel	2						2
Blackshear, Bryan	1						1
Banister, Henry	1						1
Boykin, Samuel	2						2
Bowen, William	1						1
Barkley, James	2						2
Taliaferro's							
Brown, John F.	2						2
Brown, Thomas C.	1						1
Brown, Edwards	2						2
Boykin, James	2						2
Babb, William	2						2
Brown, Mildred		1					1
Brown, Mildred for orphans of John Brown					1		1

Bevin, John	1							1
Borland, William	2							2
Marshall's								
Calhoun, James S.	1							1
Cook, Benjamin	2							2
Crow, Thomas S.	2							2
Cooper, John M.	2						1	3
Cook, Joseph	2							2
Collier, John	2							2
Cumbest, John	2							2
Clements, Thomas	1							1
Christian, Charles	2							2
Clark, William B.	2					2		4
Cooper, William	1							1
Collier, Richard	2							2
Cline, Abram	2							2
Corry, James	1							1
Cary, Edward	2							2
Cone, Samuel	2							2
Coleman, Sophiah		1						1
Coleman, Sophia for orphan of Elliot Coleman					1			1
Craft, Hugh	1							1
Cook, Isaac	2							2
Crenshaw, William H.	2							2

Corey, John	2						2
Christian, Elijah W.	1						1
Taliaferro's							
Chapman, Berry S.	1						1
Chambliss, William	1						1
Callaway, John	2						2
Callaway, Jacob	1						1
Callaway, John	2						2
Chapman, Isaiah	2						2
Chandler, Sarah		1					1
Chandler, Sarah for orphans of Danl Chandler				1			1
Marshall's							
Doster, Joshua	1					2	3
Doster, Malachi	1						1
Daniel, William J.	1						1
Davis, William	1						1
Dannelly, Arthur S.	1						1
Dannelly, Thomas	2						2
Dyer, Eliphalet C.	1						1
Daud, Amasa	1						1
Darnel, Henry for orphans of Jo^{sh} Steele				1			1
Taliaferro's							
Dickson, Thomas	2						2

Doyle, Dennis	2							2
Deracan, Hiram M.	2							2
Dubose, John	1							1
Dubose, Elias	1							1
Dubose, Peter	2							2
Marshall's								
Everett, Silas	2							2
Easter, John C.	2							2
Elliott, Andrew	2							2
Ellington, Elizabeth		1						1
~~Eugene, William J.~~							1	1
Easter, Mary		1						1
Taliaferro's								
Edwards, William L.	2							2
Eilands, Nancy		1						1
Eilands, Nancy for orphans of Isaiah Eilands					1			1
Marshall's								
Ferrell, Salley		1						1
Ferrell, Bryant orphan					1			1
~~Fair, Peter~~						1		1
Finn, Greenberry	1							1
Felps, Robert A.	1							1
Fort, Zachariah C.	1							1
Fleming, James	2							2

Fleming, Laird	1						1
Francisco, John	1						1
Fort, Tomlinson	1						1
Freeman, Martha		1					1
Freeman, Martha for orphan of Fred Freeman				1			1
Freeney, William B.	1						1
Taliaferro's							
Freeman, Joseph	1						1
Freeney, Rebecah		1					1
Freeney, Rebecah for orphans of Gillah Freeney				1			1
Franklin, Esom D.	2						2
Franklin, Esom D. for orphan of David Triplett				1			1
Franklin, Sampson	1						1
Freeman, William	2						2
Freeman, William for orphan of John Freeman				1			1
Freeman, Friend	1						1
Marshall's							
Greene, John	1						1
Gray, Priscilla		1					1
Griffin, John	1						1
Gent, Peter	2						2
Goodall, Samuel	2						2

Greene, Rhodam A.	1							1
Gates, Thomas J.	1							1
Groves, John	1							1
Gamble, James	2							2
Glenn, James	1							1
Griggs, Rhodom S.	1							1
Griggs, Leroy P.	1							1
Glover, Mark	1							1
Glass, Nancy for orphans of John McKean					1			1
Goodwin, Mathew	2							2
Goolsby, Samuel	1							1
Greene, William	2							2
Griffin, William	1						2	3
Taliaferro's								
Garner, Reddick	2							2
Goode, James	1							1
Griggs, Thomas	1							1
Greenlee, Samuel	1							1
Godwin, Simeon M.	1							1
Marshall's								
Holt, Thaddeus C.	1							1
Holt, Thaddeus C. for orphans of Thaddeus Holt (to wit) Caroline S. & Fowler Holt					1			1

Holcombe, Henry B.	2							2
Harper, Mary		1						1
Harper, Mary for orphans of Solomon Harper						1		1
Harrison, James	1							1
Howel, Sarah for orphans of Daniel Howel						1		1
Huckaby, Brittain	2							2
Hammond, Abner	2							2
Harris, Drury							1	1
Holt, Milton	1							1
Hussar, Felix	1							1
Hood, William	1							1
Hammond, Daniel	2							2
Humphrey, Hardy P.	2							2
Howard, Edy		1						1
Howard, John, Sen[r]	2							2
Howard, John H.	2							2
Hargrove, Laban	1							1
Hughes, Anna		1						1
Haas, Henry, of Cap[t] Dozier's District	2							2
Haas, Henry for orphans of John Dawson						1		1
Haas, Henry for orphans of Dan[l] McDaniel						1		1

Harper, Mary		1				1
Taliaferro's						
Hodges, Abel	2					2
Hicks, John H.	2					2
Huchinson, William	2					2
Hicks, Sarah		1				1
Hoy, Clinton	2					2
Hicks, Daniel	2					2
Marshall's						
Jones, Walter	2					2
Jones, Seaborn	2					2
Jones, Ezra B.	1					1
~~Jones, Joseph~~ Jones, Ezra B. for orphans of Joseph B. Jones	1			1		1
Jordan, Overoff	2					2
Jordan, Hezekiah by O. Jordan	2					2
Jeter, Francis	2					2
Jarrett, Patterson	2					2
Jarrett, William D.	2					2
Jarrett, Patterson for orphans of Devereaux Jarrett				1		1
Jarrett, Rebecah		1				1
Jones, Frances		1				1

Johnston, John	1							1
Jowell, Ratcliff	1							1
Jenkins, Polley W.		1						1
Jailett, Peter F.	2							2
Jones, John A. for orphans of Fleming Grantland					1			1
John A. Jones for Eliza Grantland		1						1
Jowell, Richard	2						2	4
Johnston, Nicholas	1							1
Taliaferro's								
Johnston, Samuel	2							2
Jones, Gabriel	2							2
Jones, John	1							1
Jones, William	1							1
Johnston, Sarah		1						1
Marshall's								
Ketler, Mildred					1			1
Knight, Thomas	1							1
King, George W.	2							2
King, George W. for orphans of James Howard					1			1
Kramer, David	2							2
Kenan, Thomas H. for orphan of Nathan Powell					1			1
Taliaferro's								

Kirkpatrick, James	1							1
Kilpatrick, David	2							2
King, Hannah		1						1
King, Hannah for orphans of Levi King					1			1
Kraatz, John	2							2
Marshall's								
Lucas, John	1							1
Lewis, William	2							2
Lewis, Fauntleroy	1							1
Lane, Edmund for orphans of Thos D. Clark					1			1
Logan, Philip	2					2		4
Logan, Philip for orphans of Hugh Logan					1			1
Langford, Edmund	2							2
Langford, Edmund for orphans of John Burden					1			1
Lacruse, Francis	2							2
Locke, Abner, Guardian for Elizabeth & Obedience Lowe					1			1
Locke, Abner, Guardian for Washington Dawson					1			1
Locke, Abner	1							1
Locke, Mary		1						1
Locke, Mary for orphan of Jonathan Locke					1			1

Lindsey, William	1								1
Lunsford, Rolen	1								1
Lucas, John, merch[t]	2								2
Lucas, Kezia		1							1
Lucas, John for orphans of James Lucas					1				1
Lenos, Charles	2								2
Lewis, Elizabeth		1							1
Lewis, William for orphan of Jn° Lewis					1				1
Lewis William, agent for Augustin Lewis of Hancock County of Captain Mim's District	2								2
Lee, Salley		1							1
Lee, Salley for orphans of John McLee					1				1
Lamar, C. Q. Lucius	2								2
Taliaferro's									
Leonard, Benjamin	2								2
Leonard, Joseph	1								1
Lacey, John B.	1								1
Leonard, John	2								2
Marshall's									
McGehee, George					1				1
Morgan, Richard M.	1								1
Malone, Henry W.	1								1

Moss, James	1							1
Moss, Epps	1							1
Moncrief, Sterling	1							1
McCarty, Cornelius	2							2
Micklejohn, Robert	1							1
Musclewhite, William	1							1
Murphy, Daniel	2							2
Murphy, Ellis	1							1
Murphy, Drury	1							1
Miles, Meadows	1							1
Marsh, Hesther		1						1
Marsh, Hesther for orphans of Eli Marsh					1			1
McMillan, Daniel	1							1
Meacham, James	1							1
McGehee, Samuel	1							1
Moore, Bartholomew B.	1							1
Malone, Charles	2							2
Martin, William	1							1
McCoy, Alexander	1							1
Marcus, Thomas	2							2
Murden, Mildred		1						1
Murden, Mildred for orphan of Jeremiah Murden					1			1
Mitchell, John	1							1

Moffit, Gabriel C.	1							1
McDaniel, Samuel	1							1
Mitchell, John	1							1
Marshall, James	1							1
Taliaferro's								
Molpus, Jeremiah	2						2	4
Montgomery, James	2							2
Montgomery, James for orphans of Berry Patillo						1		1
Minor, Mary		1						1
Minor, Mary for orphans of John B. Minor						1		1
Moran, John	2							2
Moran, William	2							2
Moran, Jesse	1							1
Moran, Frances		1						1
Moran, Frances for orphan of Elisha Moran						1		1
Morris, Obediah	2							2
Morris, Obediah for orphan of Ephraim Moore						1		1
Martin, Ailey		1						1
Martin Ailey for orphans of David Martin						1		1
Martin, William	1							1
Miller, Nathaniel	2							2

Miller, Nathaniel for orphan of Joseph T. Slade					1			1
Marshall's								
Nipper, William	1							1
Neeley, Richard	1							1
Newsom, Anthony	1							1
Orme, Richard M.	1							1
Owens, Anne		1						1
Taliaferro's								
O'Daniel, Alexander	1							1
Marshall's								
Pike, Polley		1						1
Pike, Polley for orphans of Nathaniel Pike					1			1
Pierce, Lovick, Senr	2							2
Pelham, Edward	1							1
Preswood, Robert	2							2
Pulliam, William	1							1
Porter, Samuel	2							2
Perry, Willis	1							1
Proctor, Martha R.		1						1
Paschal, Dennis	1							1
Parr, James	1							1
Philips, Benjamin							1	1
Pryor, Marlow	2							2

Pace, David	1							1
Taliaferro's								
Pulley, Benjamin	2							2
Pride, John	2							2
Marshall's								
Robertson, William	2							2
Richards, Christopher C.	1							1
Rutherford, Robert	2							2
Redding, William C.	1							1
Rucker, Mary Anne		1						1
Rucker, Mary Anne for orphan of George Rucker					1			1
Rowe, Chancey	1							1
Rucker, Jane for orphans of Willis Rucker					1			1
Raford, Patience		1						1
Rousseau, James	2							2
Ray, William	1							1
Ratclif, George	1							1
Reid, John	1							1
Reid, William	2							2
Reid, Templeton	1							1
Rona, Joseph	1							1
Taliaferro's								
Robinson, Solomon	2							2

Robinson, Luke	1							1
Robinson, William	1							1
Robinson, John R.							1	1
Marshall's								
Stubbs, Thomas B.	2							2
Saunders, Stephen	2							2
Sturges, Daniel	2							2
Stovall, Joseph					1	1		2
Stovall, Joseph	2							2
Sanford, Frederick	2							2
Stephens, Simeon L.	1							1
Stanford, James	2							2
~~Swan, Salley~~		0						0
~~Salley Swan for orphan of Ebenezer Swan~~						0		0 Jr
Stubbs, Baradell P.	1							1
Spencer, Alonson	2							2
Salter, Richard	1							1
Stone, Michael	2							2
Scurlock, Daniel	1							1
Sims, Benjamin	1							1
Stubbs, Peter	1							1
Stoughtenburg, Peter B.	1							1
Sturges, Benjamin H.	1							1
Simpson, John	2							2

Stone, William D.	2							2
Shackleford, Edmund	2							2
Smith, John	1							1
Sanford, Jess of Taliaferro's District	2							2
Taliaferro's								
Summerton, Thomas	2							2
Steeley, James	2							2
Smith, John R.	2							2
Simpson, George	2							2
Smith, James	1							1
Smith, Sarah		1						1
Slaughter, Daniel	2							2
Marshall's								
Trapp, Thomas	2							2
Terondet, James C.	1							1
Trapp, Phillip	1							1
Thornton, Henry	2							2
Trapp, Thomas Guardian for Joseph Sims, orphan						1		1
Thomas, George	1							1
Tulley, John A.	1							1
Taliaferro's								
Turner, Joshua	2							2
Tucker, Joseph	2							2

Turner, Milborn	1							1
Taylor, Martha		1						1
Taylor, Martha for orphans of William Taylor						1		1
Taliaferro, Richard C.	2							2
Thomas, David	2							2
Thomas, Sherrod	1							1
Tompkins, Jane		1						1
Tompkins, Jane for orphans of Wm Tompkins						1		1
Marshall's								
Vickers, Vincent E.	1							1
Vickers, Nancy		1						1
Vass, John M.	2							2
Williams, Anderson	2							2
Weeks, William	1							1
Ware, John H.	1							1
Williams, John	1							1
Wall, Eliza	1	1						1
Washington, Robert B.	2							2
Washington, Robert B., Junr	1							1
Watson, Robert	1							1
Watson, Caty		1						1
Weatherly, William	2							2
Willey, Leroy M.	1							1

Willey, Leroy M. for orphans of Moses Wiley					1				1
Whitaker, Simon	2								2
Winget, Amos	2								2
Watson, Allen	1								1
Wilson, James	2								2
Ware, William W.	1								1
Wright, Charlton	1								1
Watson, Alexander, Jun	1								1
Wright, Pryor	2								2
Wright, John H.	2								2
Wiseman, John	2								2
Whallis, Francis	2								2
Wright, William	1								1
Wood, Elisha	1								1
Willis, William	1								1
Woodall, Archibald	2								2
Williamson, Charles	2								2
Williamson, Eugene J.								1	1
Wooten, John for orphans of Joseph Selby					1			1	2
Taliaferro's									
Winget, Richard B.	2								2
Worsham, Jeremiah	2								2
Winget, Michael	2								2

Welch, William	2						2
Winget, Emmanuel	1						1
Wheeler, David	2						2
Willowby, John	1						1

County Copy of Marshall's and Taliaferro's Districts

The following transcription is from the third item on the second microfilm roll and contains the County Copy of the lists for the militia districts commanded by Captains Marshall and Taliaferro. On the front cover of the original volume is printed the words, "Milledgeville District." Presumably a clerk, either when compiling the list or soon thereafter, added the words "Taliaferros &" above the printed words, and "Lottery" beneath. based upon the handwriting and writing instrument employed, some added the words

> (older than the two preceding books)

As previously noted, the Milledgeville District was commanded by Captain Marshall during this period and was referred to by both names. No column headings or militia district names appear on any page of the original volume; but, based upon a comparison with the State Copy, Captain Marshall's District appears on the lefthand pages and Captain Taliaferro's District appears on the righthand pages. The columns also appear to be the same as those for the State Copy. The names of the applicants are arranged in approximate alphabetical order by the first letter of their surnames.

On the last page of the original volume, a clerk made the following notations.

John A. Jones

~~Hughes, James, Irwins Dist., 2 draws~~

~~Ogden, Solomon, Captain Irwins District, 4 draws~~

R. Rutherford 122

~~Geo. W. King 75~~

~~Trapp 25~~

~~Smith, Sarah, Taliaferros District, 1 Draw, Widow~~

Marshall's								
Atkinson, Littleton	1							1
Allen, Harris	2							2
Allen, John	2							2
Ayers, William	1							1
Taliaferro's								
Austin, John	1							1
Akridge, John	1							1
Akridge, Abel	2							2
Allen, Cousie		1						1
Marshall's								
Blithe, J. Anne					1			1
Bird, Thompson	2							2
Bird, John C.	1							1
Bridggers, James C.	1							1
Boon, John	2							2
Betts, Elisha	2							2
Brown, John U.	2							2
Britton, Harriet		1						1
Britton, Harriet for orphans of John Britton					1			1
Boon, William	1							1
Brown, Phebe		1						1
Brown, Phebe for orphan of William Brown					1			1

Betton, Solomon	2							2
Brown, Samuel							1	1
Barron, Joseph	2							2
Buchannan, H. L. Revinus	1							1
Ball, William	2							2
Bozeman, John	2							2
Barrow, James, Senr	1							1
Bevin, William	2							2
Bevin, William for orphans of Shadrack Bevin					1			1
Brown, William	2							2
Burgy, Henry	2							2
Bower, Bennannuel	1							1
Burden, Elizabeth		1						1
Baxter, Thomas W.	2							2
Barrow, Jacob	2							2
Barrow, Jacob for orphan of Moses Barrow					1			1
Betton, Charles F. M.	1							1
Brady, Nathan, Junr	1							1
Bowles, David	1							1
Bevin, William	1							1
Bradford, Thomas M.	1							1
Berry, James	1							1
Beckam, Absalon B.	1							1

Bulger, Daniel	2						2
Bush, Henry	1						1
Bowers, Arthur	2						2
Bozeman, James	2						2
Barrow, William	1						1
~~Brown, Thomas C.~~	1						1
~~Babb, William~~	2						2
Bostwick, Anne		1					1
Bostwick, Anne for orphans of Chesley Bostwick					1		1
Buffington, Samuel	2						2
Blackshear, Bryan	1						1
Banister, Henry	1						1
Boykin, Samuel	2						2
Bowen, William	1						1
Barkley, James	2						2
Taliaferro's							
Brown, John F.	2						2
Brown, Thomas C.	1						1
Brown, Edwards	2						2
Boykin, James	2						2
Babb, William	2						2
Brown, Mildred		1					1
Brown, Mildred for orphans of John Brown					1		1

Bevin, John	1						1
Borland, William	2						2
Marshall's							
Calhoun, James S.	1						1
Cook, Benjamin	2						2
Crow, Thomas S.	2						2
Cooper, John M.	2					1	3
Cook, Joseph	2						2
Collier, John	2						2
Cumbest, John	2						2
Clements, Thomas	1						1
Christian, Charles	2						2
Clark, William B.	2				2		4
Cooper, William	1						1
Collier, Richard	2						2
Cline, Abram	2						2
Corry, James	1						1
Cary, Edward	2						2
Cone, Samuel	2						2
Coleman, Sophiah		1					1
Coleman, Sophia for orphan of Elliot Coleman				1			1
Craft, Hugh	1						1
Cook, Isaac	2						2
Crenshaw, William H.	2						2

Corey, John	2							2
Christian, Elijah W.	1							1
Taliaferro's								
Chapman, Berry S.	1							1
Chambliss, William	1							1
Callaway, John	2							2
Callaway, Jacob	1							1
Callaway, John	2							2
Chapman, Isaiah	2							2
Chandler, Sarah		1						1
Chandler, Sarah for orphans of Danl Chandler					1			1
Marshall's								
Doster, Joshua	1						2	3
Doster, Malachi	1							1
Dannelly, William J.	1							1
Davis, William	1							1
Dannelly, Arthur S.	1							1
Dannelly, Thomas	2							2
Dyer, Eliphalet C.	1							1
Doud, Amasa	1							1
Darnel, Henry for orphans of Jo^{sh} Steele					1			1
Taliaferro's								
Dickson, Thomas	2							2

Doyle, Dennis	2							2
Deracan, Hiram M.	2							2
Dubose, John	1							1
Dubose, Elias	1							1
Dubose, Peter	2							2
Marshall's								
Everett, Silas	2							2
Easter, John C.	2							2
Elliott, Andrew	2							2
Ellington, Elizabeth		1						1
~~Eugene, William J.~~							1	1
Easter, Mary		1						1
Taliaferro's								
Edwards, William L.	2							2
Eilands, Nancy		1						1
Eilands, Nancy for orphans of Isaiah Eilands					1			1
Marshall's								
Ferrell, Salley		1						1
Ferrell, Bryant orphan					1			1
~~Fair, Peter~~							1	1
Finn, Greenberry	1							1
Felps, Robert A.	1							1
Fort, Zachariah C.	1							1
Fleming, James	2							2

Fleming, Laird	1							1
Francisco, John	1							1
Fort, Tomlinson	1							1
Freeman, Martha		1						1
Freeman, Martha for orphan of Fred Freeman					1			1
Freeney, William B.	1							1
Taliaferro's								
Freeman, Joseph	1							1
Freeney, Rebecah		1						1
Freeney, Rebecah for orphans of Gillah Freeney					1			1
Franklin, Esom D.	2							2
Franklin, Esom D. for orphan of David Triplett					1			1
Franklin, Sampson	1							1
Freeman, William	2							2
Freeman, William for orphan of John Freeman					1			1
Freeman, Friend	1							1
Marshall's								
Greene, John	1							1
Gray, Priscilla		1						1
Griffin, John	1							1
Gent, Peter	2							2
Goodall, Samuel	2							2

Greene, Rodham A.	1							1
Gates, Thomas J.	1							1
Groves, John	1							1
Gamble, James	2							2
Glenn, James	1							1
Griggs, Rhodom S.	1							1
Griggs, Leroy P.	1							1
Glover, Mark	1							1
Glass, Nancy for orphans of John McKean					1			1
Goodwin, Mathew	2							2
Goolsby, Samuel	1							1
Greene, William	2							2
Griffin, William	1						2	3
Taliaferro's								
Garner, Reddick	2							2
Goode, James	1							1
Griggs, Thomas	1							1
Greenlee, Samuel	1							1
Godwin, Simeon M.	1							1
Marshall's								
Holt, Thaddeus C.	1							1
Holt, Thaddeus C. for orphans of Thaddeus Holt (to wit) Caroline S. & Fowler Holt					1			1

Holcombe, Henry B.	2							2
Harper, Mary		1						1
Harper, Mary for orphans of Solomon Harper					1			1
Harrison, James	1							1
Howel, Sarah for orphans of Daniel Howel					1			1
Huckaby, Brittain	2							2
Hammond, Abner	2							2
Harris, Drury							1	1
Holt, Milton	1							1
Hussar, Felix	1							1
Hood, William	1							1
Hammond, Daniel	2							2
Humphrey, Hardy P.	2							2
Howard, John H.	2							2
Hargrove, Laban	1							1
Hughes, Anna		1						1
Haas, Henry, of Capt Dozier's District	2							2
Haas, Henry for orphans of John Dawson					1			1
Haas, Henry for orphans of Danl McDaniel					1			1
Harper, Mary		1						1
Taliaferro's								

Hodges, Abel	2						2
Hicks, John H.	2						2
Huchinson, William	2						2
Hicks, Sarah		1					1
Hoy, Clinton	2						2
Hicks, Daniel	2						2
Marshall's							
Jones, Walter	2						2
Jones, Seaborn	2						2
Jones, Ezra B.	1						1
~~Jones, Joseph~~ Jones, Ezra B. for orphans of Joseph Jones	1				1		1
Jordan, Overoff	2					2	4
Jordan, Hezekiah by his father Overoff Jordan	2						2
Jeter, Francis	2						2
Jarrett, Patterson	2						2
Jarrett, William D.	2						2
Jarrett, Patterson for orphans of Devereaux Jarrett					1		1
Jarrett, Rebecah		1					1
Jones, Frances		1					1
Johnston, John	1						1
Jowell, Ratcliff	1						1

Jenkins, Polley W.		1						1
Jailett, Peter F.	2							2
Jones, John A. for orphans of Fleming Grantland					1			1
John A. Jones for Eliza Grantland		1						1
Jowell, Richard	2						2	4
Johnston, Nicholas	1							1
Taliaferro's								
Johnston, Samuel	2							2
Jones, Gabriel	2							2
Jones, John	1							1
Jones, William	1							1
Johnston, Sarah		1						1
Marshall's								
Ketler, Mildred S.					1			1
Knight, Thomas	1							1
King, George W.	2							2
King, George W. for orphans of James Howard					1			1
Kramer, David	2							2
~~Kenan, Thomas H. for orphans of Nathan Powell~~					~~1~~			~~1~~
Kraatz, John	2							2
Taliaferro's								
Kirkpatrick, James	1							1

Kilpatrick, David	2							2
King, Hannah		1						1
King, Hannah for orphans of Levi King					1			1
Marshall's								
Lucas, John	1							1
Lewis, William	2							2
Lewis, Fauntleroy	1							1
Lane, Edmund for orphans of Thos D. Clark					1			1
Logan, Philip	2					2		4
Logan, Joel	1							1
Logan, Philip for orphans of Hugh Logan					1			1
Langford, Edmund	2							2
Langford, Edmund for orphans of John Burden					1			1
Lacruse, Francis	2							2
Locke, Abner, Guardian for Elizabeth & Obedience Lowe, orphans of O. Lowe					1			1
Locke, Abner, Guardian for Washington Dawson, orphan of John Dawson					1			1
Locke, Abner	1							1
Locke, Mary		1						1
Locke, Mary, for Jesse Locke, orphan of Jonathan Locke					1			1

Lindsey, William	1							1
Lunsford, Rolen	1							1
Lucas, John, merch[t]	2							2
Lucas, Kezia		1						1
Lucas, John for orphans of James Lucas					1			1
Lenos, Charles	2							2
Lewis, Elizabeth		1						1
Lewis, William for orphan of Jn° Lewis					1			1
Lewis, William, agent for Augustin Lewis of Hancock County of Captain Mim's District	2							2
Lee, Salley		1						1
Taliaferro's								
Leonard, Benjamin	2							2
Leonard, Joseph	1							1
Lacey, John B.	1							1
Leonard, John	2							2
Lee, Sally, for orphans of John McLee, Marshall's District					**1**			**1**
Marshall's								
McGehee, George					1			1
Morgan, Richard M.	1							1
Malone, Henry W.	1							1

Moss, James	1					1
Moss, Epps	1					1
Moncrief, Sterling	1					1
McCarty, Cornelius	2					2
Micklejohn, Robert	1					1
Musclewhite, William	1					1
Murphy, Daniel	2					2
Murphy, Ellis	1					1
Murphy, Drury	1					1
Meadows, Miles	1					1
Marsh, Hesther		1				1
Marsh, Hesther for orphans of Eli Marsh				1		1
McMillan, Daniel	1					1
Meacham, James	1					1
McGehee, Samuel	1					1
Moore, Bartholomew B.	1					1
Malone, Charles	2					2
Martin, William	1					1
McCoy, Alexander	1					1
Marcus, Thomas	2					2
Murden, Mildred		1				1
Murden, Mildred for orphan of Jeremiah Murden				1		1
Mitchell, John	1					1

Moffit, Gabriel C.	1							1
McDaniel, Samuel	1							1
Mitchell, John	1							1
Marshall, James	1							1
Taliaferro's								
Molpus, Jeremiah	2					2		4
Montgomery, James	2							2
Montgomery, James for orphans of Berry Patillo					1			1
Minor, Mary		1						1
Minor, Mary for orphans of John B. Minor					1			1
Moran, John	2							2
Moran, William	2							2
Moran, Jesse	1							1
Moran, Frances		1						1
Moran, Frances for orphan of Elisha Moran					1			1
Morris, Obediah	2							2
Morris, Obediah for orphan of Ephraim Moore					1			1
Martin, Ailey		1						1
Martin, Ailey for orphans of David Martin					1			1
Martin, William	1							1
Miller, Nathaniel	2							2

Miller, Nathaniel for orphan of Joseph L. Slade					1			1
Marshall's								
Nipper, William	1							1
Neeley, Richard	1							1
Newsom, Anthony	1							1
Orme, Richard M.	1							1
Owens, Anne		1						1
Taliaferro's								
O'Daniel, Alexander	1							1
Marshall's								
Pike, Polley		1						1
Pike, Polley for orphans of Nathaniel Pike					1			1
Pierce, Lovick, Sen[r]	2							2
Pelham, Edward	1							1
Preswood, Robert	2							2
Pulliam, William	1							1
Porter, Samuel	2							2
Perry, Willis	1							1
Proctor, Martha R.		1						1
Paschal, Dennis	1							1
Parr, James	1							1
Philips, Benjamin							1	1
Pryor, Marlow	2							2

Pace, David	1							1
Taliaferro's								
Pulley, Benjamin	2							2
Pride, John	2							2
Marshall's								
Robertson, William	2							2
Richards, Christopher C.	1							1
Rutherford, Robert	2							2
Redding, William C.	1							1
Rucker, Mary Anne		1						1
Rucker, Mary Anne for orphan of George Rucker						1		1
Rowe, Chauncey	1							1
Rucker, Jane for orphans of Willis Rucker						1		1
Raford, Patience		1						1
Rousseau, James	2							2
Ray, William	1							1
Ratclif, George	1							1
Reid, John	1							1
Reid, William	2							2
Reid, Templeton	1							1
Rona, Joseph	1							1
Taliaferro's								
Robinson, Solomon	2							2

Robinson, Luke	1								1
Robinson, William	1								1
Robinson, John R.								1	1
Marshall's									
Stubbs, Thomas B.	2								2
Sanders, Stephen	2								2
Sturges, Daniel	2								2
Stovall, Joseph's orphans				1	1				2
Stovall, Joseph	2								2
Sanford, Frederick	2								2
Stephens, Simeon L.	1								1
Stanford, James	2								2
~~Swan, Salley~~		0							0
~~Salley Swan for orphan of Ebenezer Swan~~					0				0 Jr
Stubbs, Baradell P.	1								1
Spencer, Alonson	2								2
Salter, Richard	1								1
Stone, Michael	2								2
Scurlock, Daniel	1								1
Sims, Benjamin	1								1
Stubbs, Peter	1								1
Stoughtenburg, Peter B.	1								1
Sturges, Benjamin H.	1								1
Simpson, John	2								2

Stone, William D.	2							2
Shackleford, Edmund	2							2
Smith, John	1							1
Sanford, Jess of Taliaferro's District	2							2
Taliaferro's								
Summerton, Thomas	2							2
Steeley, James	2							2
Smith, John R.	2							2
Simpson, George	2							2
Smith, James	1							1
Smith, Sarah		1						1
Slaughter, Daniel	2							2
Marshall's								
Trapp, Thomas	2							2
Terondet, James C.	1							1
Trapp, Phillip	1							1
Thornton, Henry	2							2
Trapp, Thomas Guardian for Joseph Sims orphan						1		1
Thomas, George	1							1
Tulley, John A.	1							1
Taliaferro's								
Turner, Joshua	2							2
Tucker, Joseph	2							2

Turner, Milborn	1							1
Taylor, Martha		1						1
Taylor, Martha for orphans of William Taylor					1			1
Taliaferro, Richard C.	2							2
Thomas, David	2							2
Thomas, Sherrod	1							1
Tompkins, Jane		1						1
Tompkins, Jane for orphans of Wm Tompkins					1			1
Marshall's								
Vickers, Vincent E.	1							1
Vickers, Nancy		1						1
Vass, John M.	2							2
Williams, Anderson	2							2
Weeks, William	1							1
Ware, John H.	1							1
Williams, John	1							1
Wall, Eliza	1	1						1
Washington, Robert B.	2							2
Washington, Robert B., Junr	1							1
Watson, Robert	1							1
Watson, Caty		1						1
Weatherly, William	2							2
Willey, Leroy M.	1							1

Willey, Leroy M. for orphans of Moses Wiley					1			1
Whitaker, Simon	2							2
Winget, Amos	2							2
Watson, Allen	1							1
Wilson, James	2							2
Ware, William W.	1							1
Wright, Charlton	1							1
Watson, Alexander, Jun	1							1
Wright, Pryor	2							2
Wright, John H.	2							2
Wiseman, John	2							2
Whallis, Francis	2							2
Wright, William	1							1
Wood, Elisha	1							1
Willis, William	1							1
Woodall, Archibald	2							2
Williamson, Charles	2							2
Williamson, Eugene J.							1	1
Wooten, John for orphans of Joseph Selby					1		1	2
Taliaferro's								
Winget, Richard B.	2							2
Worsham, Jeremiah	2							2
Winget, Michael	2							2

Welch, William	2							2
Winget, Emmanuel	1							1
Wheeler, David	2							2
Willowby, John	1							1

Irwin's and Stephen's Districts

As previously noted, the following transcription is from the State Copy on the first roll of microfilm and includes the the militia districts commanded by Captains Irwin and Stephens. From the microfilm images, the lists appear to be contained in a separate original volume. On the first lefthand page, the clerk wrote the following column headings.

Captain Stephens District Names of Applicants

Applicants Generally

Widows

Widows of persons who died in the public Service during the late War

Orphans of persons who died in the public Service during the late wars

Orphans Generally

Revolutionary Officers & Soldiers

Persons who Served in the late Seminole War

Total

On the opposite righthand page, the clerk wrote the same column headings for Captain Irwin's District. The actual lists, in approximate alphabetical order by the first letter of each surname, appear on subsequent pages without any column headings.

Stephens'					
Anderson, Abijah	2				2
Akridge, Joseph E.	1				1
Akridge, William	2				2
Akridge, Ezekiel					1
Britt, Obed	2				2
Box, Mary for orphans of Shadrach Box				1	1
Brooks, Ivy	1				1
Brooks, John Z.	1				1
Bateman, James	2				2
Brooks, Simon	2				2
Bailey, Henry	2				2
Brooks, Maxey	1				1
Irwin's					
Beasley, Charles	1				1
Burgess, Samuel	2				2
Barrow, Henry	2				2
Beckum, Laban	2				2
Bevins, Thomas	1				1
Beckum, Laban for orphans of Allen Beckum				1	1
Beckum, Laban for orphans of Robert Weeker				1	1
Bowers, Benjamin	2				2
Bowers, Jesse	2				2

Brown, Mark M.	2							2
Bickers, John	2							2
Brown, William P.	2							2
Bevin, Milley		1						1
Branham, Thomas	2							2
Stephens'								
Chapman, John D.	2							2
Castlebury, Thomas	2							2
Cobb, Joseph, Senr	1							1
Cobb, Benjamin	1							1
Cobb, Mark	1							1
Chapman, Mary		1						1
Cobb, Darling	1							1
Cobb, Joseph, Junr	1							1
Chambliss, Zachariah for orphans L. Gardiner					1			1
Crabtree, John	2							2
Clements, Mathew	1							1
Cox, Willis	1							1
Chambliss, John	1							1
Chambliss, Alexander	1							1
Cox, Zilpha		1						1
Cox, Zilpha for orphans of Henry Cox					1			1
Irwins'								

Clark, John, Gen[l]	2						2
Crowder, John M.	2						2
Carter, Mary		1					1
Carter, Mary for orphans of Thomas Carter				1			1
Colbert, William	1						1
Cay, William	2						2
Chancellor, William	2						2
Chancellor, John	1						1
Stephens'							
Davis, Toliver	2						2
Douglass, Jones	2						2
Digby, Nathaniel	1						1
Davis, John	1						1
Ethridge, Marmaduke	2						2
Ethridge, Caleb	2						2
Fuller, John	2						2
Irwins'							
Driver, John	2						2
Dadd, Isaac	2						2
Edge, John	2						2
Edge, John for orphans of Joseph Digby				1			1
Fletcher, Joseph	2						2
Stephens'							

Greene, Richard	2							2
Greene, Amos	1							1
Gafford, Thomas	1							1
Gafford, John	1							1
Gafford, Hannah		1						1
Gafford, Hannah for orphans of John Gafford					1			1
Greene, Benjamin	1							1
Griffin, Andrew	2							2
Gailord, Giles	1							1
Howard, John	2							2
Hill, David B.	2							2
Hill, David B. for orphans of Robert Hill					1			1
Harwell, William	1							1
Harris, Sarah		1						1
Harris, Sarah for orphans of Thomas Harris					1			1
Harris, Mary	1							1
Harwell, Sarah	1							
Irwin's								
Grigg, William	2							2
Grigg, William for orphans of Jonathan McCrary					1			1
Gilbert, Josiah	2							2
Guerry, Theodore	2							2

Gilbert, Josiah for orphans of David Harrison					1		1
Hoy, William	2						2
Hoy, William, Junr	1						1
Harvey, John H.	2						2
Herring, George	2						2
Herring, Charlotte for orphans of Lemuel Wilson					1		1
Hughes, James	2						2
Hammond, Abner	2						2
Stephens'							
Jones, Francis	2						2
Joiner, Mary		1					1
Justice, Levi	2						2
Joiner, Joseph	1						1
Joiner, Absalom	1						1
Justice, Dempsey	2						2
Johnston, Caleb	2						2
Lee, Thomas	2						2
Lesueur, Drury M.	2						2
Long, Evans for orphans of Nathaniel Pritchard					1		1
Long, Nimrod W.	1						1
Irwin's							
Jordan, William B.	1						1
Irwin, James	2						2

Irwin, James for orphans of Daniel Triplet					1		1
Kennon, William	2						2
Lewis, John T.	1						1
Lowe, Obediance		1					1
Stephens'							
Maxcy, Nathaniel	2						2
Maddox, Abigail		1					1
McCullen, Rachel		1					1
Maxcy, Henry Thomas	1						1
Maxcy, David A.	1						1
Maddox, Benjamin	2						2
McCrary, John	2						2
McCrary, John for orphans of Isaac McCrary					2		2
McKinney, George	2						2
McDonold, Absalom	1						1
Irwin's Dis[t]							
Mobley, John	1						1
Miller, Nathaniel A.	1						1
Miller, Ezekiel	2						2
Martin, Edmund	2						2
Minter, Anthony	2						2
Miller, William	2						2
McComack, Catren		1					1

McCrary, Hannah for orphans of Jon. McCrary					1		1
Miller, Jesse	2						2
McCrary, Bartley, Sen[r]	2						2
McCrary, Bartley, Jun	2						2
Miller, Ezekiel Guardian for orphans of Abel James					1		1
Miller, Bazel for orphans of Charles Williamson					1		1
Mims, Seaborn	2						2
Mims, Seaborn for orphans of Shadrach Mims					1		1
Moore, Margaret		1					1
Moore, Margaret for orphans of Thomas Moore					1		1
Moseley, Joseph						1	1
McCrary, James	1						1
McCrary, Mathew	1						1
McCrary, Robert	1						1
Martin, Morris	2						2
McCrary, Willie	1						1
Moses, Neil	1						1
Martin, John	1						1
Minter, James	2						2
Mims, Needham	2						2
Mims, Needham for orphans of John Cox					1		1

Mims, Needham for orphans of John Mims					1			1
Miles, William	1							1
McCrary, Hannah		1						1
Stephens'								
Owens, John J.	2							2
Owens, John J. for orphans of Elijah Owens					1			1
Perry, Michael W.	2							2
Perry, Nicholas	2							2
Rogers, Cannon R.	2							2
Irwin's								
Ogden, Solomon	2							2
Parker, Elisha, Junʳ	2							2
Pasmore, John	2							2
Parker, Martha		1						1
Parker, Martha for orphans of John Parker					1			1
Petigrew, James	2							2
Parker, Henry	1							1
Powell, James	1							1
Perry, Obed	1							1
Ready, Isham	2							2
Ready, Ursley		1						1
Ready, Ursley for orphans of John Ready					1			1

Rains, Allen	2						2
Riddle, Willie	2						2
Ready, Spotswood G.	2						2
Rutherford, Williams	2						2
Stephens'							
Stephens, John	2						2
Stephens, Isaac	1						1
Stephens, Lewis	1						1
Sledge, Alexander	2						2
Smith, John H.	2						2
Smith, Charles	2						2
Sharp, John	2						2
Swillivant, Elijah	2						2
Terry, Nathaniel	2						2
Taurence, Amelius	2						2
Taurence, Esther		1					1
Taurence, Esther for orphans of Andrew Taurence					1		1
Taylor, William D.	1						1
Turk, Thomas	2						2
Turner, Henry	2						2
Taylor, Eden	2						2
Taurence, Mansfield	1						1
Irwin's							

Scott, John, Genl	2							2
Scott, Thomas Bayless	1							1
Stinson, William	1							1
Sheffield, Bartley	2							2
Strickland, Archibald	2							2
Snipes, Jonathan	1							1
Smith, William Thomas	2							2
Shelby, Evans	2							2
Steele, Elizabeth		1						1
Steele, Elizabeth for orphans of Sampson Steele					1			1
Snow, Salley for orphans of Ebenezer Snow					1			1
Snow, Salley		1						1
Terry, Richard	2							2
Troutman, John	2							2
Trapp, Timothy	2							2
Troutman, Hiram	1							1
Tapley, Joel	2							2
Thompson, William	2							2
Thompkins, John	2							2
Thompson, James	2							2
Stephens'								
Wallace, Enoch	2							2
Worsham, Archer, Junr	2							2

Worsham, Daniel B.	2						2
White, Rachel		1					1
Williams, Mary		1					1
Williams, Mary for orphans of John Williams					1		1
Williams, Thomas	2						2
Wicker, John	1						1
Worsham, David G.	1						1
Wilkerson, Malcomb G.	2						2
Whitaker, Mark	2						2
White, William	2						2
Worsham, Archer, Sen[r]	2						2
Worsham, Archer, Sen for orphans of David Worsham					1		1
Worsham, Patrick H.	1						1
White, John	2						2
Worsham, John G.	2						2
Irwin's							
Underwood, Enoch	2						2
~~Underwood, Enoch for orphans of Tilman Britain~~ bloted out by Spec request					~~1~~		~~1~~
Williamson, Randol	1						1
White, Beersheba		1					1
Willis, Robert	1						1
Willis, Williamson	2						2

Willis, Price	2							2
Woolsey, Benjamin	2							2
Willis, Keziah		1						1
Willis, Keziah for orphans of Robert Willis					1			1
Willis, Britton	1							1
Wooton, John	2							2
Wilkerson, Nancy		1						1
Wilkerson, Nancy for orphans of Sherod Wilkerson					1			1
Young, Amos	2							2

Georgia, Baldwin County }

I hereby Certify that the foregoing list is a correct return as far as I know of persons entitled to draws in the contemplated Land Lottery of Captains Marshalls, Stephens, Irwins, & Taliaferros districts. The left hand page Containing Captains Marshalls & Taliaferros districts & the right page containing Captains Irwins & Stephens districts agreeable to the caption intended for each page.

Fr. Jeter

Baldwin County

Fortunate Drawers

The following transcription is from the third, and last, item on the first microfilm roll and contains the names of those fortunate enough to win land in the lottery. The list of fortunate drawers is in tabular format, with six columns, the first column the name of the fortunate drawere, the second and third columns the fortunate drawers county and militia district of residence, the fourth column the land lot number, the fifth and sixth columns the land district and county where the land lot was located. The names are arranged in approximate alphabetical order by the last leter of the surname.

Name	County	District	Lot	Dist	County
Harris Allen	Baldwin	Marshalls	368	27	Early
Littleton Atkinson	Baldwin	Marshalls	123	12	Hall
Joseph Anders	Baldwin	Cousins	400	15	Early
John Atkerson, S[r]	Baldwin	Haws	291	3	Early
John Allums	Baldwin	Cousins	193	1	Irwin
John Atkerson, S[r]	Baldwin	Haws	3	3	Appling
Abijah Anderson	Baldwin	Stephens	126	6	Early
Harris Allen	Baldwin	Marshalls	297	8	Appling
William Akridge	Baldwin	Stephens	47	5	Gwinnett
John Austin	Baldwin	Taliaferros	457	3	Appling
Nathaniel Ashton	Baldwin	Marshalls	115	8	Hab[r]
Barksdale Terrell	Baldwin	Doziers	306	15	Early
Jacob Barron	Baldwin	Marshall	50	3	Early
William Bowen	Baldwin	Marshall	374	13	Early
Jacob Barrentine	Baldwin	Doziers	116	1	Irwin

Name	County	District	Lot	Dist	County
Joshua D. Bostwick	Baldwin	McCrarys	277	28	Early
Allen Beckham's orps	Baldwin	Irwins	157	1	Walton
Mildred Brown	Baldwin	Taliaferros	494	3	Appling
Joseph Bowen	Baldwin	Marshalls	327	12	Irwin
Jesse Bowers	Baldwin	Irwins	57	7	Gwinnett
Henry Brewer	Baldwin	Cousins	200	20	Early
James C. Bridgers	Baldwin	Marshalls	496	5	Appling
Revinus H. L. Buchannan	Baldwin	Marshalls	519	2	Appling
Maxey Brooks	Baldwin	Stephens	438	13	Irwin
Robert Blair	Baldwin	Marshalls	256	7	Gwinnett
Henry Bartow	Baldwin	Marshalls	62	4	Appling
John M. Brown	Baldwin	Marshalls	335	10	Irwin
Absalom B. Beckham	Baldwin	Marshalls	298	5	Irwin
William Babb	Baldwin	Taliaferros	56	4	Walton
James Bevins	Baldwin	Ellis	254	17	Early
John Boon	Baldwin	Marshalls	146	3	Appling
Thomas M. Bradford	Baldwin	Marshalls	361	1	Early
Nancy Boler, wid	Baldwin		65	1	Early
Daniel Bulger	Baldwin	Marshalls	306	14	Early
John Britton's orps	Baldwin	Marshalls	205	6	Appling
Nathan Braddy, J^r	Baldwin	Marshalls	310	21	Early
Elisha Betts	Baldwin	Marshalls	79	8	Irwin
John F. Brown	Baldwin	Taliaferros	145	5	Appling

Name	County	District	Lot	Dist	County
Samuel Boykin	Baldwin	Marshalls	12	3	Irwin
David Blakey	Baldwin	Russels	240	10	Irwin
William Borland	Baldwin	Taliaferros	167	16	Irwin
James Barkley	Baldwin	Marshalls	393	12	Early
Ivey Brooks	Baldwin	Stephens	440	15	Early
David Blakey	Baldwin	Russels	240	5	Appling
~~Thomas Davis~~	Baldwin	~~Russels~~	~~458~~	~~12~~	~~Irwin~~
John					
William Boren	Baldwin	Marshalls	235	16	Early
William Barrow	Baldwin	Marshalls	81	3	Walton
Labun Beckham	Baldwin	Irwins	278	5	Irwin
Samuel Brooks	Baldwin	Doziers	326	7	Gwinnett
Edmund Brantley	Baldwin	Ellis	170	3	Appling
William P. Brown	Baldwin	Irwins	227	14	Early
Samuel Buffington	Baldwin	Marshalls	30	23	Early
Thomas Branham	Baldwin	Irwins	77	14	Irwin
James Bozeman	Baldwin	Marshalls	184	12	Irwin
John & Joel Boler orp[s]	Baldwin		62	6	Early
John Bozeman	Baldwin	Marshall's	364	8	Irwin
Edmund Brantley	Baldwin	Ellis's	215	26	Early
John Bevin	Baldwin	Taliaferros	143	21	Early
Terrell Barksdale	Baldwin	Doziers	136	8	Irwin
Jacob Barrentine	Baldwin	Doziers	153	11	Hall

Name	County	District	Lot	Dist	County
Thompson Bird	Baldwin	Marshalls	205	19	Early
Harriet Britton	Baldwin	Marshalls	326	27	Early
John F. Brown	Baldwin	Taliaferros	384	4	Appling
James Barkley	Baldwin	Marshalls	20	2	Habersham
Thomas W. Baxter	Baldwin	Marshalls	159	10	Early
Elsiha Betts	Baldwin	Marshalls	218	5	Appling
Simon Brooks	Baldwin	Stephens	79	3	Irwin
Henry Barrow	Baldwin	Irwins	71	8	Early
Joseph Booren	Baldwin	Marshalls	141	3	Early
Phebe Brown	Baldwin	Marshalls	31	12	Hall
Tandy Bealle	Baldwin	Ellis	380	12	Irwin
Thompson Bird	Baldwin	Marshalls	192	7	Gwinnett
James Bozeman	Baldwin	Marshalls	380	7	Irwin
Obed Britt	Baldwin	Stephens	176	10	Early
Henry Brewer	Baldwin	Cousins	211	21	Early
Thomas W. Baxter	Baldwin	Marshalls	448	12	Irwin
~~Castleberry, Thomas~~	Baldwin	~~Stephens~~	~~12~~	~~5~~	~~Habersham~~
Levi Cobb	Baldwin	Russels	249	2	Appling
Cook, Arthur, Jun[r]	Baldwin	Ellis'	440	4	Appling
Thomas Castleberry	Baldwin	Stephens	7	13	Habersham
Edward Carey	Baldwin	Marshall	377	21	Early
Dennis Collins	Baldwin	Cousins	527	11	Irwin
John Cumbest	Baldwin	Marshalls	206	13	Early

Name	County	District	Lot	Dist	County
John Collier	Baldwin	Marshalls	102	7	Early
John Covey	Baldwin	Marshalls	208	9	Appling
Sarah Coleman	Baldwin	Ellis'	215	5	Irwin
Henry Cook	Baldwin	Ellis'	499	13	Irwin
Cary Curry R. S.	Baldwin	Ellis	156	6	Early
William Chesher's orphs	Baldwin	Cousins	146	2	Rabin
John Chambliss	Baldwin	Stephens	66	23	Early
James Cone	Baldwin	Cousins	4	10	Irwin
Alfred Clarke	Baldwin	Russels	376	8	Irwin
Samuel Cunningham	Baldwin	Cousins	29	5	Early
John Collier	Baldwin	Marshalls	92	2	Habersham
George Cavenah	Baldwin	Ellis	71	2	Early
John Cox^s (orp^s)	Baldwin	Irwins	159	4	Appling
Matthew Clements	Baldwin	Stephens	40	5	Gwinnett
Richard Collier	Baldwin	Marshalls	52	14	Early
Berry S. Chapman	Baldwin	Taliaferro	154	7	Appling
Joseph Cook	Baldwin	Marshalls	343	28	Early
Joseph Collins	Baldwin	Cousins	67	6	Appling
Willis Cox	Baldwin	Stephens	126	2	Appling
Andrew Collins orp^n	Baldwin	Cousins'	315	6	Early
Thomas Cooper	Baldwin	Ellis'	123	3	Early
James Collins	Baldwin	Cousins	426	8	Irwin
Thomas Clower	Baldwin	Cousins	512	12	Irwin

Name	County	District	Lot	Dist	County
James Collins	Baldwin	Cousins	88	13	Early
Edm^d Chambliss (son of Zachariah)	Baldwin	Stephens'	113	12	Hall
George Cavenah	Baldwin	Ellis'	53	9	Hall
Isaiah Chapman	Baldwin	Taliaferros	234	10	Irwin
Mary Carter	Baldwin	Irwins	383	5	Early
Sarah Currie	Baldwin	Russels	185	13	Irwin
W H. Crenshaw	Baldwin	Marshalls	278	12	Irwin
Edmund Cooper's (orps)	Baldwin	Cousins	525	13	Irwin
Willis Cox	Baldwin	Stephens	26	11	Irwin
Turpin Cheshers	Baldwin	Cousins	257	5	Appling
John M. Crowder	Baldwin	Irwins	243	17	Early
Elisha Curry	Baldwin	Ellis	279	12	Irwin
Elbert Calhoon	Baldwin	Doziers	119	28	Early
Cary Curry R. S.	Baldwin	Ellis	353	3	Early
William Cooper	Baldwin	Marshalls	25	5	Gwinnett
Willis Coleman	Baldwin	Ellis	151	15	Irwin
Thomas S. Crow	Baldwin	Marshalls	104	1	Habersham
Bazzel Cone	Baldwin	Haws	435	6	Appling
Dennis Collins	Baldwin	Cousins	235	7	Appling
Richard Collier	Baldwin	Marshalls	226	2	Irwin
Samuel Cunningham	Baldwin	Cousins	428	5	Appling
Charles Christian	Baldwin	Marshals	7	1	Habersham
Levin Callaway	Baldwin	Ellis	365	20	Early

Name	County	District	Lot	Dist	County
Mathew Clements	Baldwin	Stephens	86	6	Early
John Cone R. S.	Baldwin	Haws	337	18	Early
William Cook	Baldwin	Doziers	53	6	Early
Thomas Cochran	Baldwin	Haws	38	5	Irwin
Jacob Callaway	Baldwin	Taliaferros	4	11	Habersham
Hugh Craft	Baldwin	Marshals	26	1	Irwin
Dennis Doyle	Baldwin	Taliafors	78	13	Irwin
Jackey B. Dorsey	Baldwin	Cousins	45	6	Gwinnett
John Davis	Baldwin	Stevens	256	3	Early
William Davice	Baldwin	Ellis	98	3	Habersham
Toliver Davis	Baldwin	Stephens	276	5	Early
Jesse Doles R. S.	Baldwin	Cousins	207	5	Early
Thomas Dickson	Baldwin	Taliaferros	174	4	Walton
Benjamin Doles	Baldwin	Cousins	35	8	Early
Jones Douglass	Baldwin	Stephens	341	1	Appling
Isaac Dadd	Baldwin	Irwins	339	27	Early
James Durby	Baldwin	Haws	173	3	Appling
Hiram M. Deracan	Baldwin	Taliaferros	27	7	Irwin
Samuel Dentz (orps)	Baldwin	Ellis	210	6	Appling
John Dismuck's orph[s]	Baldwin	Ellis'	85	16	Irwin
Henry Densley	Baldwin	Cousins'	326	8	Appling
William Digby	Baldwin	McCrary's	86	9	Irwin
John Downer	Baldwin	Dozier	103	6	Irwin

Name	County	District	Lot	Dist	County
Hiram M. Deracan	Baldwin	Taliaferros	36	2	Appling
Amasa Doud	Baldwin	Marshall's	151	20	Early
Timothy Davis	Baldwin	Marshall's	301	6	Irwin
Malachi Doster	Baldwin	Marshall's	234	11	Irwin
Thomas Davis	Baldwin	Ellis	458	12	Irwin
Jesse Doles R. S.	Baldwin	Cousins	159	2	Appling
Joshua Doster R. S.	Baldwin	Marshalls	298	10	Irwin
Benjamin Doles	Baldwin	Cousins	89	16	Irwin
John Mims' orp[s]	Baldwin	Irwins	50	1	Walton
Washington Dawson orp[s]	Baldwin	Marshalls	317	9	Appling
Thomas Marcus	Baldwin	Marshalls	462	3	Appling
Marmaduke Ethridge	Baldwin	Stephens	338	8	Early
Thomas Evans	Baldwin	Hawes	337	7	Irwin
Marmaduke Ethridge	Baldwin	Stephens	145	5	Irwin
Thomas M. Ellis	Baldwin	Ellis	135	9	Appling
Elizabeth Ellington	Baldwin	Marshalls	254	26	Early
Caleb Ethridge	Baldwin	Stephens	295	18	Early
Isaiah Eilands' orp[s]	Baldwin	Taliaferros	15	1	Appling
William Edwards	Baldwin	Ellis's	271	4	Walton
John C. Easter	Baldwin	Marshalls	3	3	Irwin
Fielding Ellis	Baldwin	Ellis	173	1	Irwin
Andrew Elliott	Baldwin	Marshalls	323	13	Early
John Freeman's (orps)	Baldwin	Taliaferros	238	18	Early

Name	County	District	Lot	Dist	County
Gillah Freeny's (orphs)	Baldwin	Taliaferro	28	23	Early
John Fuller	Baldwin	Stephens	400	27	Early
William B. Freeny	Baldwin	Marshalls	167	5	Irwin
James Flemming	Baldwin	Marshalls	205	11	Irwin
Jones Fuller	Baldwin	Cousins	99	16	Early
Elijah Freeny	Baldwin	Russels	285	10	Early
Thompson Fields	Baldwin	Ellis	254	4	Walton
James Gleen	Baldwin	Marshall	319	6	Appling
John Henry Gault	Baldwin	Cousins	44	14	Irwin
Henry Greene	Baldwin	Cousins	516	6	Irwin
Benjamin Greene	Baldwin	Stephens	363	19	Early
Britain Ganday's (orphs)	Baldwin	Haws	32	2	Habersham
Amos Greene	Baldwin	Stephens	6	4	Habersham
Raleigh Green	Baldwin	Doziers	281	2	Appling
James Goslin	Baldwin	Doziers	90	16	Irwin
John Gafford	Baldwin	Stephens	88	5	Early
William Green (Doctor)	Baldwin	Marshalls	41	13	Habersham
Peter Gent	Baldwin	Marshalls	59	1	Appling
James Godwin	Baldwin	Russels	90	7	Early
Thomas Griggs	Baldwin	Taliaferros	43	4	Appling
Theodore Guerry	Baldwin	Irwins	31	2	Early
Hannah Gafford	Baldwin	Stephens	172	12	Habersham
Priscilla Gray	Baldwin	Marshalls	396	1	Early

Name	County	District	Lot	Dist	County
Rhodom S. Griggs	Baldwin	Marshals	331	26	Early
Thomas Gafford	Baldwin	Stephens	238	19	Early
James Gaster	Baldwin	Marshalls	53	7	Irwin
William Gill	Baldwin	Cousins	345	7	Appling
William Grigg	Baldwin	Irwins	235	11	Early
Samuel Goodall	Baldwin	Marshalls	295	28	Early
Barnet Goslin	Baldwin	Doziers	30	10	Irwin
Mark Glover	Baldwin	Marshalls	493	5	Irwin
Reddick Garner	Baldwin	Taliaferros	428	5	Appling
Andrew Griffin	Baldwin	Stephens	128	14	Early
Myles Greene	Baldwin	Doziers	133	14	Irwin
Peter Gente	Baldwin	Marshalls	207	6	Gwinnett
John Griffin	Baldwin	Marshalls	151	14	Early
David Harrison's orphans	Baldwin	Irwins	344	14	Early
Manoah Hubbard R. S.	Baldwin	Russels	294	19	Early
William Haney	Baldwin	Cousins	79	5	Appling
Brittan Huckabay	Baldwin	Marshalls	278	21	Early
Mannoah Hubbard R. S.	Baldwin	Russels	319	2	Early
William Horn	Baldwin	Ellis	270	9	Irwin
William Hoy	Baldwin	Irwins	150	3	Early
Abner Hines	Baldwin	Doziers	206	10	Early
Brittain Huckaby	Baldwin	Marshalls	90	11	Early
Eli S. Hill	Baldwin	Stephens	226	6	Appling

Name	County	District	Lot	Dist	County
John Hendricks' (orps)	Baldwin	Haws	433	7	Appling
Michael Harvey	Baldwin	Cousins	33	13	Habersham
James Horn	Baldwin	Ellis	138	11	Hall
Pleasant Hightower	Baldwin	Russels	436	5	Irwin
George Herring	Baldwin	Irwins	190	10	Early
John H. Hicks	Baldwin	Taliaferro's	294	7	Appling
Abner Hammond	Baldwin	Irwin's	160	15	Irwin
Ezekiel Harris	Baldwin	Haws	408	4	Appling
Daniel Hammond	Baldwin	Marshalls	124	8	Early
John Hamet's orp[s]	Baldwin	Doziers	373	16	Early
William Howell	Baldwin	Doziers	83	11	Early
Abner Hines	Baldwin	Doziers	122	2	Habersham
Judith Hill	Baldwin	Russels	16	5	Gwinnett
Sarah Hicks	Baldwin	Taliaferro's	255	9	Irwin
Gustavus Hendrick	Baldwin	Haws'	361	2	Early
Isham Hogan	Baldwin	Haws'	254	6	Gwinnett
Sarah Harwell	Baldwin	Stephens	5	8	Irwin
Thomas Humphries, S[r], R. S.	Baldwin	Cousins	6	7	Gwinnett
Rebecca Harvey	Baldwin	Cousins	?8	10	Habersham
Manoah Hubbard R. S.	Baldwin	Russels	80	11	Habersham
William Hightower	Baldwin	Laceys	224	8	Early
~~Daniel Howel orph~~	Baldwin	~~Marshalls~~	~~133~~	6	~~Early~~
Stephen Horton's orp[s]	Baldwin	Doziers	268	7	Irwin

Name	County	District	Lot	Dist	County
Thaddeus G. Holt	Baldwin	Marshalls	175	7	Appling
John H. Howard	Baldwin	Marshalls	107	10	Hall
Ezekiel Harris	Baldwin	Haws	384	20	Early
Henry Hunt	Baldwin	McGees	216	1	Walton
Anna Hughes	Baldwin	Marshalls	85	12	Hall
Daniel Howell's orp[s]	Baldwin	Marshalls	133	6	Early
Polley W. Jenkins	Baldwin	Marshall	139	7	Irwin
Hezekiah Jourdan	Baldwin	Marshall	38	3	Walton
Henry L. Jones	Baldwin	Ellis	404	1	Early
Loyd Johnston	Baldwin	Doziers	481	6	Appling
Dempsey Justice	Baldwin	Stephens	218	10	Early
Thomas B. Jones	Baldwin	Knights	276	11	Early
Benjamin Jenkins	Baldwin	Haws	22	13	Habersham
Benjamin Jenkins	Baldwin	Haws	334	6	Appling
John Jolly	Baldwin	Ellis	224	4	Appling
Walter Jones	Baldwin	Marshalls	131	15	Irwin
John Jolly	Baldwin	Ellis	42	5	Rabun
Levi Justice	Baldwin	Stephens	405	6	Appling
William Johnston	Baldwin	Doziers	22	6	Early
William Johnston	Baldwin	Doziers	72	3	Rabun
Samuel Johnston	Baldwin	Taliaferros	394	2	Early
Joseph B. Jones' orp[s]	Baldwin	Marshalls	204	4	Irwin
Hezekiah Jordan	Baldwin	Marshalls	351	8	Early

Name	County	District	Lot	Dist	County
Richard Jowell Rev. Sol.	Baldwin	Marshalls	138	15	Irwin
John W. Jones	Baldwin	Doziers	151	4	Irwin
Frances Jones	Baldwin	Marshalls	47	5	Irwin
Sarah Johnston	Baldwin	Taliaferros	50	12	Early
Green Jeane	Baldwin	Russels	226	19	Early
William B. Jordan	Baldwin	Irwins	258	10	Irwin
Gabriel Jones	Baldwin	Taliaferros	36	5	Appling
Seaborn Jones	Baldwin	Marshalls	34	5	Irwin
Susannah Jackson	Baldwin	Cousins	152	3	Habersham
Jacob Jackson	Baldwin	Doziers	282	4	Irwin
William D. Jarratt	Baldwin	Marshall	339	3	Early
Overoff Jordan	Baldwin	Marshalls	594	2	Appling
Seaborn Jones	Baldwin	Marshalls	357	9	Early
John A. Jones	Baldwin	Haws	67	11	Hall
Richard Jowell	Baldwin	Marshalls	25	2	Irwin
George W. King	Baldwin	Marshalls	103	5	Appling
Robert Knight's (orps)	Baldwin	Marshalls	189	4	Walton
Thomas Knight	Baldwin	Marshalls	326	12	Irwin
Maryann Kinglet (wid)	Baldwin	Marshalls	366	9	Early
Mildred Ketler	Baldwin	Marshalls	195	9	Early
William Kennon	Baldwin	Irwins	116	3	Walton
George W. King	Baldwin	Marshalls	105	3	Irwin
David Kilpatrick	Baldwin	Taliaferros	52	2	Irwin

Name	County	District	Lot	Dist	County
William Kennon	Baldwin	Irwins	22	26	Early
John Kraatz	Baldwin	Taliaferros	85	15	Early
Simeon Kemp	Baldwin	Doziers	155	27	Early
David Kramer	Baldwin	Marshalls	273	9	Irwin
Charles Lenos		Marshalls	271	9	Early
James Lester, S^r		Doziers	9	19	Early
John H. Lawson		Ellis	116	5	Early
Kezia Lucas		Marshalls	160	8	Early
Rolen Lunsford		Marshalls	176	21	Early
Phillip Logan		Marshalls	350	9	Early
Wade Lester		Haws	98	6	Appling
Edmund Low		Haws'	235	18	Early
John Lester		Haws'	128	11	Early
Hugh Logan's orp^s		Marshals	269	7	Gwinnett
Allen Little		Doziers	122	26	Early
John Little's (orphans)		Cousins	323	7	Gwinnett
John Lucas (merchant)		Marshalls	104	21	Early
William Lewis		Marshalls	505	6	Appling
Benjamin Leonard		Taliaferros	19	20	Early
John Lucas		Marshalls	26	17	Early
Isaac Lester, J^r		Haws'	81	2	Early
Drury M. Lesueur		Stephens	212	16	Early
Francis Lacruse		Marshalls	301	9	Early

Name	County	District	Lot	Dist	County
Abraham Little's (orph[s])		Doziers	90	28	Early
Phillip Logan		Marshalls	19	2	Appling
Nimrod W. Long		Stephens	192	10	Early
Isaac Lester		Haws	192	10	Irwin
Michael Leonard		Laceys	353	20	Early
Lucius Q. C. Lamar		Marshals	142	6	Early
John Little's orphin		Cousins	442	11	Irwin
Julius Lester		Haws	353	8	Appling
Hiram Lester		Haws	364	26	Early
Mitchell, D. B., Gen		Russells	153	5	Early
Cornelius McCarty		Marshall	193	10	Irwin
Morris Martin		Irwin	118	7	Gwinnett
John Myrick		Cousins	49	28	Early
Francis Mercer		Cousins	86	10	Irwin
Drury Murphy		Marshalls	63	5	Irwin
John Moran		Taliaferro	108	15	Early
Hannah McCrary		Irwins	328	11	Early
Thomas Marcus		Marshalls	21	8	Hall
Patrick Markey		Marshalls	350	21	Early
Abednego McGinty		Russels	21	6	Irwin
John Moore, J[r]		Russels	25	6	Irwin
Britton Meeks		Cousins	60	5	Irwin
George McKinnie		Stephens	271	9	Appling

Name	County	District	Lot	Dist	County
Thomas Miles		Ellis	172	5	Gwinnett
William Miller		Irwins	40	11	Irwin
Nathaniel Miller		Taliaferro	220	9	Irwin
Benjamin Martin		Haws	105	10	Early
Robert Micklejohn		Marshalls	416	3	Appling
John Myrick		Cousins	337	27	Early
James McMurry		Haws	157	10	Hall
Reps Mitchell		Marshalls	108	6	Gwinnett
John Marchman		Russells	381	11	Early
Hesther Marsh		Marshalls	284	4	Irwin
Robert McCrary		Ellis'	66	4	Walton
Wm Martin		Marshall's	119	3	Early
James McMullen		Cousins	330	12	Early
Bartley McCrary, J^r		Irwin's	9	1	Habersham
Wm Musclewhite		Marshalls	12	1	Appling
Willie McCrary		Irwins	80	7	Rabun
W^m McKinney's orph^s		Ellis'	438	6	Appling
Needham Mims		Irwins	397	1	Appling
Luke Moore		Cousins'	341	9	Early
Jesse Miller		Irwin	189	4	Irwin
Joseph Methvin		Haws	136	5	Irwin
Epps Moss		Marshalls	265	6	Appling
Samuel McGehee		Marshals	26	4	Early

Name	County	District	Lot	Dist	County
John Mobly		Irwins	179	10	Early
William Moran		Taliaferro's	243	8	Appling
Thomas Marcus		Marshalls	562	3	Appling
Samuel McDonald See Executive Order 31st August 1841		Marshalls	236	11	Early
John Maclin		Irwins	66	6	Irwin
Thomas H. Maxey		Stephens'	220	12	Irwin
Clement Moore		Haws'	212	7	Early
Elijah Moore		Haws'	239	1	Walton
Richard M. Morgan		Marshall's	48	8	Irwin
Anthony Minter		Irwins	23	3	Early
James R. McGehee		Ellis'	432	15	Early
Williamson Mims		Haws	376	8	Appling
David A. Maxey		Stephens	258	5	Early
Joseph Morris		Cousins	498	5	Appling
Edward Maclin		Irwins	5	11	Hall
James Myrick		Cousins	370	27	Early
John McCrary		Stephens	50	2	Early
Benjamin Methvin		Haws	209	7	Early
James Moran		Ellis	243	8	Appling
Archibald McDonald		Cousins	473	7	Appling
John McKean's (orphs)		Marshalls	263	4	Irwin
Obediah Morris		Taliaferros	13	4	Irwin

Name	County	District	Lot	Dist	County
Morris Martin		Irwins	321	4	Early
Thomas Moore's orp[s]		Irwins	400	13	Irwin
Mathew McCrary		Irwins	1	2	Early
William Miller		Irwins	144	21	Early
Jacob Miller		Russels	47	8	Irwin
Hiram Moore		Milledgeville	33	11	Early
Goodwin Myrick		Haws	173	8	Hall
Bartley McCrary, Jun[r]		Irwins	530	2	Appling
Jacob Miller		Russels	85	8	Appling
Robert P. Miles		Ellis	37	2	Habersham
John Mimms' orph[s]		Irwin	30	1	Walton
Bartholomew B. Moore		Marshalls	182	1	Appling
Margarett Moore		Irwins	343	11	Irwin
Thomas Morris (See Letter D)		Marshalls	467	3	Appling
Sherwood Norman		Milledgeville	32	5	Rabun
Anne Owens		Marshalls	250	13	Irwin
John J. Owens		Stephens	80	15	Early
Solomon Ogden, R. S.		Irwins	95	13	Early
Richard M. Orme		Marshals	483	2	Appling
Elijah Owens' (orphans)		Stephens	5	9	Irwin
Aaron Owens		Ellis's	182	2	Habersham
Aaron Owens		Ellis's	63	14	Early
David Pace		Marshalls	7	7	Appling

Name	County	District	Lot	Dist	County
Nicholas Perry		Stephens	213	12	Early
Obed Perry		Irwins	110	14	Early
Nathaniel Pike's (orphs)		Marshalls	128	4	Irwin
James Petigrew		Irwins	283	10	Irwin
Thomas S. Parham		Haws	192	21	Early
Nathaniel Prichard's orps		Stephens	67	6	Gwinnett
Michael W. Perry		Stephens	275	11	Early
William Peters		Haws	294	2	Appling
Samuel Porter		Marshalls	118	7	Appling
George Parker		Cousins	195	11	Irwin
Polly Parker		Ellis^s	96	1	Habersham
Jacob Parker's orp^s		Ellis^s	311	18	Early
John Pitts		Russells	153	1	Early
James A. Perdue		Haws	143	13	Early
Sarah Peters		Haws	19	17	Early
Willis Perry		Marshals	158	2	Walton
Henry Parker		Irwins	510	5	Irwin
John Peters' orphans		Haws's	6	12	Early
James A. Perdew		Haws's	335	6	Early
Wm Pulliam		Marshalls	112	12	Hall
Robertson Peters		Haws	438	28	Early
Oran D. Pearman		Doziers	1	12	Hall
Laban Pool		Ellis	269	4	Walton

Name	County	District	Lot	Dist	County
Lovick Pierce, S^r, R. S.		Marshalls	202	1	Appling
Rowland Parham		Cousins	390	7	Gwinett
James Powell		Irwins	60	3	Appling
John Parker's orp^s		Irwins	325	6	Irwin
John Pasmore		Irwins	341	5	Appling
Peter Perry		Marshalls	15	1	Rabun
Robert Preswood		Marshalls	161	3	Appling
Benjamin Pully		Taliaferros	219	28	Eary
Marlow Pryor		Marshalls	356	16	Early
Rowland Parham		Cousins	390	7	Gwinnett
William Quinn		Russels	455	3	Appling
John R. Robertson		Taliaferros	1	6	Appling
John Rice's orps		Ellis	77	9	Early
Willis Riddle		Irwins	300	11	Irwin
Cannon R. Rodgers		Stephens	41	2	Habersham
Martin Russel		Russels	341	10	Irwin
Risdon Ryan		Russels	376	28	Early
Zepheniah Reed		Ellis	18	6	Habersham
Allen Rains		Irwins	410	6	Appling
Patience Raford		Marshalls	149	14	Irwin
James Rice		Ellis	106	2	Irwin
William Robertson		Marshalls	77	6	Irwin
Christopher C. Richards		Marshalls	315	13	Irwin

Name	County	District	Lot	Dist	County
Rachael Ryan (an orphn)		Russels	611	2	Appling
William Reid		Marshalls	86	1	Appling
Nancy Rice		Ellis'	153	19	Early
Edith Redding		Doziers	37	5	Early
Thomas Redding		Doziers	152	2	Rabun
Chancey Rowe		Marshalls	213	3	Irwin
Henry Robertson		Doziers	403	3	Appling
James Rousseau		Marshalls	155	1	Appling
Christopher Rutledge's (orpns)		Cousins	463	10	Irwin
John Redding		Ellis	283	5	Appling
Templeton Reid		Marshalls	42	13	Irwin
William C. Redding		Marshalls	78	3	Walton
James Rice		Ellis	119	4	Early
William Robinson		Taliaferros	41	2	Walton
Willie Riddle		Irwins	108	7	Early
John Russel		Russels	275	7	Gwinnett
Robert Rutherford		Marshalls	8	15	Irwin
William Reid		Marshalls	147	18	Early
Sanford, Jesse		Taliaferro's	241	3	Irwin
Hubert Stephens, R. S.		Marshalls	74	3	Rabun
Cyrus Sharp		Ellis	312	13	Early
Jonathan Snipes		Irwins	116	2	Habersham
Thomas B. Stubbs		Marshalls	507	8	Irwin

Name	County	District	Lot	Dist	County
Evans Shelly		Irwins	277	19	Early
Sarah Smith		Taliaferro	323	26	Early
Ross Scott		Russels	457	9	Irwin
Richard Salter		Marshalls	390	20	Early
Bartley Shuffield		Irwins	60	10	Habersham
Simeon L. Stephens		Marshalls	238	12	Early
James Steely		Taliaferro	93	5	Early
Elijah Swillivant		Stephens	195	16	Early
Benj[a] H. Sturges		Marshalls	145	6	Irwin
James Smith's (orp[s])		Cousins	161	11	Habersham
John Stevens		Stevens	505	8	Appling
Daniel Shurlock		Marshalls	391	4	Early
William Sheppard		Haws	105	5	Gwinnett
Thomas Summerton		Taliaferro's	492	3	Appling
William Stephens		Cousins'	164	1	Walton
John Smith		Haws'	9	2	Walton
Gideon Sale		Cousins'	172	15	Early
Thomas Summerton		Taliaferros	49	12	Hall
Edmund Shackelford		Marshalls	392	8	Appling
Joseph Selby's orphans		Marshalls	67	14	Early
Joseph P. Slade's orphans		Taliaferros	333	17	Early
Bartley Sheffield		Irwins	365	5	Appling
Michael Stone		Marshalls	498	10	Irwin

Name	County	District	Lot	Dist	County
Peter Stubbs		Marshalls	495	6	Appling
John Scott, Genl.		Irwins	246	1	Walton
John Sharp		Stephens	300	6	Early
Ann Smallpeace		Doziers	394	13	Early
Jospeh S. Simpson		Laceys	74	15	Early
Joseph Sims' (orphn)		Marshalls	385	4	Early
Ebenezer Snow's (orphs)		Irwins	148	26	Early
James Stanford		Marshalls	42	4	Early
Joseph Slick's (orphan)		Marshalls	322	7	Gwinnett
Charles Smith		Stephens	362	5	Early
James Smith		Taliaferro	23	7	Irwin
Charles Sheppar's (orph)		Cousins	430	2	Appling
James Thompson		Irwins	199	7	Appling
Timothy Trapp		Irwins	112	18	Early
Joshua Turner		Taliaferros	432	3	Appling
John Tomkins		Irwins	83	11	Habersham
Samuel Tarentine		Cousins	487	6	Appling
Nathaniel Terry		Stephens	104	6	Irwin
John Troutman		Irwins	605	2	Appling
Timothy Trapp		Irwins	7	4	Appling
Joseph Tucker		Taliaferro	312	12	Early
John Troutman		Irwins	514	6	Appling
Henry Thornton		Marshalls	373	1	Appling

Name	County	District	Lot	Dist	County
Nathaniel Terry		Stephens	393	9	Early
Thomas Turk		Stephens	51	16	Irwin
Daniel Tripplett's (orps)		Irwins	346	13	Irwin
Henry Thompson		Doziers	431	6	Irwin
William Thompson		Irwins	51	7	Appling
James Thompson		Irwins	127	12	Early
Benjamin Talbott, R. S.		Cousins'	179	16	Early
William Taylor's orp^s		Taliaferros	185	14	Early
John Tompkins		Irwins	53	5	Irwin
Shelburn Turner		Taliaferroes	130	15	Early
William D. Taylor		Stephens'	278	4	Early
Henry Turner		Stephens'	28	10	Early
David Thomas		Taliaferros	385	28	Early
Spencer Thomas, J^r		Haws	223	9	Irwin
William Thompson		Irwins	245	8	Appling
James Thomas		Russels	59	6	Early
John A. Tully		Marshals	15	6	Appling
Spencer Thomas, Senr		Haws	326	1	Appling
Joshua Turner		Taliaferro	69	10	Early
Gracy Thomas		Haws	75	5	Rabun
Benjamin Talbot, R S.		Cousins	56	8	Early
Enoch Underwood		Irwins	166	8	Early
Enoch Underwood		Irwins	88	21	Early

Name	County	District	Lot	Dist	County
Hatcher Vickers		Marshalls	47	15	Irwin
Benjamin Vincent		Ellis'	186	3	Irwin
Alexander Varner		Ellis'	40	8	Irwin
John M.. Vass		Marshalls	227	6	Early
Wright, John H.		Marshall's	393	1	Appling
Benedick White		Cousins	16	2	Early
Robert B. Washington (June)		Marshalls	75	10	Hall
Alexander Watson		Cousins	144	9	Early
John Wood's (orps)		Haws	227	7	Early
Archer Worsham (Junr)		Stephens	94	9	Early
Alexander Watson, Jun		Marshalls	292	27	Early
Abednego Wright		Russels	443	6	Irwin
James C. Watson		Cousins	125	7	Gwinnett
Anderson Williams		Marshalls	33	1	Appling
John Wicker		Stephens	211	19	Early
Robert B. Washington		Marshalls	496	9	Irwin
William C. Watson		Cousins	15	2	Appling
Eugene J. Williamson		Marshalls	145	6	Early
Enoch Wallace		Stephens	346	7	Early
Green Wommack Altered by Ex order of Decr 10th 1836		Cousins	397	4	Appling
Archer Worsham, S^r		Stephens	122	4	Habersham
William Willis		Marshall's	178	12	Irwin

Name	County	District	Lot	Dist	County
Lemuel Wilson's (orps)		Irwins	105	9	Irwin
William Welch		Taliaferro	243	4	Walton
Archer Worsham, J^r		Stephens	12	13	Habersham
Francis Whallis		Marshal's	257	7	Irwin
Charles Willingham		Cousins'	348	5	Appling
Williamson Willis		Irwins	427	1	Appling
James C. Watson		Cousins'	115	5	Early
Benedict White		Cousins'	256	9	Irwin
Charles Williamson		Marshal's	171	16	Early
Michael Wingate		Taliaferros	17	16	Irwin
Daniel B. Worsham		Stephens	52	4	Early
Jesse Wheeler		Cousins'	161	1	Appling
James Willingham		Cousins'	204	28	Early
William Welch		Taliaferro's	68	7	Early
John Windham		Ellis'	171	10	Early
Michael Wingate		Taliaferro's	94	22	Early
Benjamin Woolsey		Irwins	54	4	Irwin
Eli Works		Ellis's	91	5	Early
Sherod Wilkinson's orp^s		Irwins	50	12	Irwin
Samuel Watson		Cousins'	82	9	Appling
Winfrey Williams		Haws'	153	12	Hall
Francis Whallis		Marshals	174	11	Irwin
William Weeks		Marshals	233	16	Early

Name	County	District	Lot	Dist	County
Simon Whitaker		Marshalls	245	2	Appling
Nancy Wilkerson		Irwins	172	10	Early
Simon Whitaker		Marshalls	72	27	Early
Mark Womack		Doziers	169	10	Irwin
Robert Warren		Doziers	447	4	Appling
Mark Whitaker		Stephens	485	7	Irwin
Price Willis		Irwins	298	3	Early
Thomas Williams		Stephens	307	7	Irwin
Mary Williams		Stephens	115	2	Rabun
John Williams		Milledgeville	136	14	Early
Robert B. Washington		Marshals	516	8	Appling
Malcom G. Wilkinson		Stephens	110	7	Appling
James Wilson		Marshalls	343	8	Early
John Windham		Ellis	294	7	Irwin
David Wheeler		Taliaferro	153	11	Irwin
Elisha Wood		Marshalls	281	6	Appling
Archibald Woodall		Marshalls	202	9	Appling
Thomas Young		Harris	182	16	Irwin
Amos Young		Irwins	102	13	Irwin
Willis Yates		Russels	307	21	Early
Turner Young's (orps)		Harris	465	7	Appling
Benjamin Yarborough		Marshalls	520	13	Irwin

1821 Land Lottery

On May 16, 1821, Governor John Clark signed the legislation authorizing the 1821 Land Lottery, titled

An Act to dispose of and distribute the lands lately acquired by the United States for the use of Georgia, of the Creek Nation of Indians, by a treaty made and concluded at the Indian Spring, on the eighth day of January, eighteen hundred and twenty-one; and to add the reserve at Fort Hawkins to the county of Jones.

The act established five new counties in the ceded lands, Dooley, Fayette, Henry, Houston, and Monroe, and authorized the Surveyor General to divide each county into numbered land districts and each land district into numbered lots, as follows.

County	Land Districts	Lot Sizes
Dooley	Districts 1-16	202 ½ acres
Fayette	Districts 6, 7, 9, and 14	202 ½ acres
Henry	Districts 1-18	202 ½ acres
Houston	Districts 1-16	202 ½ acres
Monroe	Districts 1-15	202 ½ acres

The eligibility requirements specified by the legislation were nearly identical to those of the previous lottery.

- Bachelor, 18 years or older, 3-year residence in Georgia, 3-year citizen United States – 1 draw
- Married man with wife or son under 18 years or unmarried daughter, 3-year residence in Georgia, 3-year citizen United States – 2 draws
- Widow, 3-year residence in Georgia – 1 draw
- Family of minor orphans, father dead, 3-year residence in Georgia – 1 draw
- Family (one or two) of orphans under 21 years, father and mother dead – 1 draw
- Family (three or more) of orphans under 21 years, father and mother dead – 2 draws

- Widow, husband killed or died in Revolutionary War, War of 1812, or Indian War, 3-year residence in Georgia – 2 draws
- Orphan, father killed or died in Revolutionary War, War of 1812, or Indian War – 2 draws
- Child or family of children of a convict, 3-year residence in Georgia – entitled in the same manner as orphans

The act excluded from participation in the lottery

- Any fortunate drawer in any previous land lottery.
- Citizens of the state who volunteered or were legally drafted during the War of 1812 or Indian War and refused to serve a tour of duty in person or by substitute.
- Any convict in the penitentiary.
- Any tax defaulter or absconder for debt.

The procedure of administering and performing the lottery was substantially the same as in the previous lottery. The act required each person to take an oath substantiating their eligibility and pay 25 cents per draw before their name could be entered, but the cost of each grant was $19. Again, the lottery employed two large wheels to conduct the lottery, one filled with a number of tickets equal to the total number of draws, on which the name of the drawer, their county and militia district of residence, and any other identifying information, was written by hand, and the second wheel filled with the same number of tickets, printed either with the land lot number, land district, and county, or the word blank. The actual lottery drawing commenced November 7, 1821 and ended December 12, 1821.

On October 23, 1821, the following notice appeared in the *Georgia Journal*, published at Milledgeville.

> *Executive Department, Georgia*
> *Milledgeville, 15th October, 1821*
> *The Commissioners of the Land Lottery being convened at this place for the purpose of making the necessary preparations for the same, having informed the Executive that from the progress made, they think they shall be in readiness to proceed to the drawing of said Lottery on the 6th of November next.*

Notice is therefore given in pursuance of the latter part of the 17th section of the act of the General Assembly of this State, passed 15th of May last, that the drawing of said Lottery will commence at this place on the 6th day of the ensuing month. By order of the Governor,

Elisha Wood, Sec'ry

The editors of the Georgian, the Darien Gazette, the Georgia Advertiser, the News, at Washington, and the Athens Gazette, are requested to give the above two insertions in their respective papers.

Major Amos Young's Battalion

The following transcription is from the first item on the second microfilm roll and contains the lists for the five militia districts comprising the Battalion District commanded by Major Amos Young. On the spine of the original record volume are the printed words, *Land Lottery 1821 – Baldwin County*.

On the inside front cover of the original volume, a clerk wrote

1941
Verified by Nancy Hart Chapter D. A. R.

On the first page of the original record volume, the clerk wrote

The following is a list of persons names who are entitled to Draw in the next contemplated Land Lottery, which are authorized by an act of the Legislature of the State of Georgia, at an extra Session, held in April & May, in the year 1821 in the Town of Milledgeville for Major Amos Young's Battalion, Baldwin County.

    N° of Captains Districts

    Capt Huson's is no 320
    Capt McCrarey's is no 321
    Capt Malcolm's is no 429
    Capt Stephenses is no 322
    Capt White's is no 115

Captain Russel's District in Major R. W. Ellises Battalion is N° 105

1821

The list is consists of a table with three columns, the first column containing the name of the applicant and any identifying remarks recorded by the clerk, the second column the militia district where the applicant resided, and the thrird column the total number of draws to which the applicant was entitled.

Immediately underneath the name Howell King, someone placed a question mark within parentheses. Whether that someone was a clerk, a member of the D. A. R., or someone else, and whether the notation was placed when the original list was compiled or at some late date, entirely uncertain.

Apparently, the applicants who resided in Captain White's District appear in the following table, in spite of their not being a part of Major Young's Battalion.

Applicant's Name and Remarks	Captain's District	Draws
John Allen	Husons	2
James L. Askew	Husons	1
Joseph E. Akridge	Stephens	1
Abraham Ayers	Whites	2
Laborn Armstrong	Whites	1
William J. Andrews	Husons	1
Eli Abbott	McCrareys	2
William Ayers	Malcolms	1
William B. Akridge	McCrareys	1
Wiley Armstrong	Husons	2
John Allen	Whites	1
Cuzza Allen (widow)	Whites	1
William Bressie	Husons	2
William Brown	Malcolms	2
James Barrow, Senior	Husons	2
Benjamin Bowers	McCrareys	2
Loam Brown	McCrareys	2
Robert Brown	McCrareys	2
Samuel H. Burgess	Malcolms	2
James Barrow, Junior	Husons	1
William Ball	Husons	2
Milley Bivins (widow)	McCrareys	1
For minor orphans of Shadrach Bivins	McCrareys	1

Applicant's Name and Remarks	Captain's District	Draws
Rolen Bivins	McCrareys	2
Mary Box (widow)	Stephens	1
Lemmons Box	Stephens	1
Hiram Brooks	Stephens	1
James Bateman	Stephens	2
John Z. Brooks	Stephens	2
Shadrach Boxes orphans	Stephens	1
Benanuel Bower	Malcolms	2
James Boykin	Whites	2
William Bivins	Malcolms	2
Chloe Bozeman (widow)	Malcolms	1
Uriah Brown	McCrareys	2
Manassa Brown	McCrareys	1
James N. Bozeman	McCrareys	1
Elizabeth Brown, orphan	Malcolms	1
Samuel Brown	Malcolms	1
James Bryant	McCrareys	1
Thomas Bivins	McCrareys	1
John Burch	Husons	2
Drewcillar Brown (widow)	Whites	1
Richard G. Brown's orphans	Whites	1
James Berry	Malcolms	1
Thomas C. Benning	Husons	1

Applicant's Name and Remarks	Captain's District	Draws
Rowanna E. & Sarah F. Browning, orphans	Husons	1
Timothy Bruen	Husons	2
Leroy Boothe	Malcolms	1
Albert G. Beckham	Malcolms	1
William Brown, Senior	McCrareys	1
Maxy Barnes	Husons	1
Ann Bostick (widow)	Husons	1
Chesley Bostick's orphans	Husons	1
John Bedingfield, orphan	Husons	1
William Belding	Husons	1
David W. Bowles	Husons	1
Benagah Boothe	Malcolms	1
John G. Bird	Husons	1
Solomon Betton	Malcolms	2
John Calaway	Whites 115	2
Andrew Coney	Whites	1
William Cay	McCrareys	2
John Cay	McCrareys	1
Isaac Copland	Husons	1
William B. Clark	Malcolms	2
James Camak	Malcolms	2
Benjamin Cobb	Stephens	1
Jacob Cobb	Stephens	1

Applicant's Name and Remarks	Captain's District	Draws
Darling Cobb	Stephens	1
Mark Cobb	Stephens	1
Joseph Cobb	Stephens	1
Robert R. Cumming	Malcolms	1
William L. Candler	Whites	1
Daniel Candler's orphans	Whites	1
Philip Cook	Husons	2
Abram Cline	Husons	2
Polley Cocks' (orphan)	McCrareys	1
John Clark	Stephens	1
Reubin Cloud	Nunns	2
Henry Chappell	Nunns	1
Samuel Chappell	Nunns	1
John T. Carter	Nunns	1
Joel Crawford	Nunns	1
Isaac T. Cushing	Malcolms	2
Bushrod Crowder	McCrareys	1
John Callaway	Whites	2
Hiram Crowder	McCrareys	1
Daniel Colvin	Malcolms	1
Sarah Callaway (widow)	Whites	1
Elisha Callaway's orphan	Whites	1
Zilpha Cox (widow)	Stephens	1

Applicant's Name and Remarks	Captain's District	Draws
Henry Coxes orphans	Stephens	1
James Covey	Husons	1
By certificate		
Elisha Cushing	McCrareys	1
George T. Dortic	Husons	1
Arthur Danelly	Whites	2
John P. Davanne	Husons	1
Jane Dean (widow)	Stephens	1
William Dean's orphans	Stephens	1
Esau Davis	Stephens	2
Cross R. Davis	McCrareys	1
James Dean	Stephens	1
Jesse Davis	Stephens	1
Peter Dubose, Senior	Whites	2
William Dickson	Whites	1
Owen Duffy	Husons	1
Thomas Dyer	Malcolms	2
Eliphalet Dyer	Malcolms	1
Mary Davis (widow)	Stephens	1
Arthur B. Davis	Husons	1
John Dees	McCrareys	2
William J. Danelly	Malcolms	1
By certificate	Hawses E. B.	1

Applicant's Name and Remarks	Captain's District	Draws
John Darby	Hawses E. B.	1
Joseph Digby's orphans by Williams	McGehees E. B.	2
John Ethridge	Stephens	2
Allen Estes	Stephens	2
John Ethridge's orphans	Stephens	1
William B. Edwards	McCrareys	1
Nancy Evans (widow)	Husons	1
Mary Easter (widow)	Malcolms	1
Nancy Eilands (widow)	Whites	1
William L. Edwards	Whites	2
Charles H. French	McCrareys	2
Laird Fleming	Husons	1
John Fleming	Stephens	1
Lenidas Few	Husons	1
Joseph Freeman	Whites	1
Wyatt Foard	Husons	2
John Francisco	Husons	1
Tomlinson Fort	Malcolms	1
Frederick Freeman's orphans	Malcolms	1
William Freeman	Whites	2
Ignatius Few's orphans	Husons	1
Esam D. Franklin	Whites	2
Simpson Franklin	Whites	1

Applicant's Name and Remarks	Captain's District	Draws
Sarah A. Ferell (widow)	Malcolms	1
Mary Ann B. Ferell orphan	Malcolms	1
Isaac Golden	McCrareys	2
Abraham Golden	McCrareys	2
John P. Gordon	Husons	1
Samuel G. Good	Whites	1
James S. Good	Whites	1
James Gamble	Husons	2
John R. Golden	Malcolms	1
Elias F. Gardener	Husons	1
William L. Greene	Husons	1
Rhodom A. Greene	Husons	1
Susan T. Greene, orphan	Husons	1
Seaton Grantland	Husons	2
Eliza A. Grantland (widow)	Husons	1
Fleming Grantland's orphans	Husons	1
Sarah Greene (widow)	Husons	1
Simeon Godwin	Whites	2
Archibald B. Graham	Husons	1
Wright Grooms	Husons	1
John Gorman	Husons	1
Marcus D. Huson (Captain)	Husons 320th	1
William Hoy	McCrareys	2

Applicant's Name and Remarks	Captain's District	Draws
John H. Harvey	McCrareys	2
James Howard's orphans, by George W. King	Husons	1
Henry B. Holcombe	Husons	2
Thomas Harris' orphans	Stephens	1
Daniel Hicks	Whites	2
William Huchinson	Whites	2
Abel Hodges	Whites	2
William G. House	Whites	2
Thomas Huson	Husons	2
David B. Hill	Stephens	2
Robert Hill's orphan	Stephens	1
Samuel Harvill	Stephens	1
Elias Harriss	Husons	2
Eadeth Howard (widow)	Malcolms	1
Laban Hargrove	Husons	1
Jesse Hargrove	Husons	1
Hardy P. Humphrey	Husons	2
Eli W. Harrison	Malcolms	1
William & Thomas Hill, by their mother	Russels, Elliss Bat	1
William Hollingsworth	Malcolms	2
Allbas W. Harris	Husons	1
John B. Hines	Husons	1

Applicant's Name and Remarks	Captain's District	Draws
Larkin Holcolmbe	Whites	1
Ellen G. C. Harris, orphan, by mother	Malcolms	1
John Haley	Husons	2
George Haas	Husons	2
Thomas Higgans	Husons	2
By certificate		
Anderson Holt	Malcolms	1
Mathew J. Jordan	McCrareys	1
Ezra B. Jones	Husons	1
Rebecca F. Jarratt (widow)	Husons	1
Absolam Joyner	Stephens	2
Luke Jackson	Stephens	2
Robert Ivey	Stephens	2
Turna Ivey	Stephens	1
Joseph Joyner	Stephens	2
Barna Ivey	Stephens	2
James Jones	Whites	1
Green B. Jackson	Husons	1
Mary Joyner (widow)	Stephens	1
John Jones	Stephens	2
Sarah Johnson (widow)	Husons	1
Devereaux Jarratt's orphans	Husons	1
Mark M. R. Jewell	Malcolms	1

Applicant's Name and Remarks	Captain's District	Draws
Francis Jeter	Malcolms	2
James A. Jeter	Malcolms	1
George Irvin	McCrareys	1
Cannon Jones	Whites	2
Paterson Jarratt	Husons	2
Peter F. Jaillet	Husons	2
Thomas J. Kirkpatrick	Whites	1
Leonard Kimbrough	McCrareys	2
Lewis H. Kenan	Husons	1
Peter W. Kimbrell	Husons	1
Hardy H. Kenan	Husons	1
Elizabeth Kraatz (widow)	Malcolms	1
John Kraatz' orphans	Malcolms	1
John Kennington	McCrareys	2
Howel King (?)	Husons	1
William Lindsey	Whites 115	1
Joseph Leonard	Whites	1
John T. Lewis	McCrareys	1
Ulysses Lewis	Husons	1
Edmund Lankford	Husons	2
Jesse Ladd	Husons	1
Archibald Lee	Stephens	1
Jordan B. Lesueur	Stephens	2

Applicant's Name and Remarks	Captain's District	Draws
Harrison Lesueur	Stephens	1
Richard T. Lingo	Whites	1
Thomas Lumpkin	Husons	1
William Lingold	McCrareys	2
Robert Lassiter	Husons	1
Mary Locke (widow)	Husons	1
Jesse Locke	Husons	1
Fielding Lewis	Husons	1
Obediance Lowe (widow)	McCrareys	1
Obadiah Lowe's orphans	McCrareys	1
Daniel Lyman	Husons	1
Joseph S. Loving	Husons	1
Elizabeth Lewis (widow)	Husons	1
Sarah Lee (widow)	Malcolms	1
John Leonard	Whites	2
Abner Locke	Husons	1
Owen Myrick	Whites 115	2
Ellis Murphey	Malcolms	1
Ezekiel Miller	McCrareys	2
William J. Maclin	McCrareys	1
Jonathan A. Miller	McCrareys	1
Robert McCrarey	McCrareys	1
James McCrarey, Capt. 321	McCrareys	1

Applicant's Name and Remarks	Captain's District	Draws
Bartley McCrarey, Senior	McCrareys	2
William McCrarey's orphans, by Bartley McCrarey, J^r, Adm^r	McCrareys	1
John Malcolm, Captain 429	Malcolms	2
James McKnight	Husons	1
John Miller	Husons	1
~~Rebecca Jarrat (widow)~~	~~Husons~~	~~1~~
Jonathan McCrarey	Stephens	1
Neal Moses	Stephens	1
Joseph Maddox	Stephens	2
Jesse Moore	McCrareys	2
Henry W. Malone	Malcolms	2
Thomas Moore	Whites	2
Mary Minor (widow)	Whites	1
John B. Minor's orphans	Whites	1
Mary Morris (widow)	Whites	1
Jesse Maynor	Malcolms	2
James Montgomery	Whites	2
Josiah McGinty	Husons	1
Malcom McLeod	Husons	1
William Martain	Husons	1
John Munrow	Malcolms	1
Daniel Munrow's orphans, father & mother both dead	Malcolms	2

Applicant's Name and Remarks	Captain's District	Draws
Cornelius Murphy	McCrareys	1
Gideon Mims	McCrareys	1
Hiram Mann	Malcolms	1
Daniel Murphy	Malcolms	2
Edward M. Murphy	Malcolms	1
James Minter	Malcolms	2
Abigal Maddox (widow)	Stephens	1
July Murden, orphan of Jeremiah Murden	Malcolms	1
Jourdan S. Murray	Husons	1
John Mitchell	Malcolms	1
Jonathan McCrarey's orphans	McCrareys	1
William Miles	McCrareys	1
Reddick Massengale	McCrareys	2
Zacheus Mager	Husons	1
Eli Marshes orphans	Malcolms	1
James Meacham	Husons	1
Redding Musselwhite	Malcolms	1
James Moore	McCrareys	2
Jesse Moran	Whites	2
Alay Martain (widow)	Husons	1
David Martain's orphans	Husons	1
John Minter	Husons	1
Frances Moran (widow)	Whites	1

Applicant's Name and Remarks	Captain's District	Draws
Elizabeth Moran, orphan	Whites	1
Alexander McGregor	Malcolms	2
Isaac McCrarey's orphans, father & mother dead	Stephens	2
Abram A. Massias	Husons	1
Rachel McColours (widow)	Stephens	1
Robert Northcutt's orphans, whose father & mother are dead	Malcolms	2
Isaac Newell	Malcolms	1
Alexander O'Daniel	Whites 115	1
John Oliver	McCrareys	1
John Oler	Whites	2
Martha Parker (widow)	McCrareys	1
Charles J. Paine	Husons	2
Hugh W. Proudfoot	Husons	1
Narcissa Pertilla, orphan	Whites	1
John E. Perryman &	Husons	1
for Savility Perryman, orphan	Husons	1
Abel Pearson	Husons	1
Jetson Perry	McCrareys	1
Joseph Porvin	Stephens	1
Stephen Pardee	Husons	1
John Pride	Whites	2
Jesse Prosser	Whites	2

Applicant's Name and Remarks	Captain's District	Draws
Leonard Perkins	Malcolms	1
William Puryear	Husons	2
Tamsey T. Pine (widow)	Husons	1
Solomon Perry	Malcolms	1
~~Elizabeth~~		
John D. Pitts	Whites	2
John Puckett	Malcolms	2
Josephus Reid	Malcolms	1
Williams Rutherford	McCrareys	2
Simon P. Robinson	Husons	1
Ursley Ready (widow)	McCrareys	1
John Ready's orphans	McCrareys	1
Mariah Roys (widow)	Malcolms	1
Samuel Rockwell	Husons	2
James T. Rives' orphans	Husons	1
Alexander Richards	Husons	2
Spotwood G. Ready	McCrareys	2
Thomas Rousseau	Husons	1
James M. Simpson	Whites 115	1
Baradell P. Stubbs	Husons	1
David Stutes	Husons	1
Joseph Stovall	Husons	2
Frederick Sanford	Husons	2

Applicant's Name and Remarks	Captain's District	Draws
Jacob Skinner	Husons	1
Peter B. Stoutenburgh	Malcolms	1
William Sentell	Stephens	2
Elizabeth Steele (widow)	Stephens	1
Sampson Steele's orphans	Stephens	1
Esley Sharp	Stephens	1
Isaac Stephens	Stephens	1
Lewis Stephens, Captain	Stephens N° 322	2
Alexander Sledge	Stephens	2
John H. Smith	Stephens	2
Stephen W. Snow's orphans	Malcolms	1
Synadonia Snow (widow)	Malcolms	1
John R. Smith	Whites	2
Thomas Stackpole	Malcolms	2
William Stinson	McCrareys	2
Stephen Sanders	Husons	2
Daniel Sturges	Malcolms	2
James Sparrow	Husons	1
John Smith	Husons	1
Sarah Snow (widow)	Husons	1
Benjamin A. Sims	Husons	1
Frances Slaughter (widow)	Whites	1
Frances G. Slaughter, orphan	Whites	1

Applicant's Name and Remarks	Captain's District	Draws
Amilius Torrance	Stephens	2
William H. Torrance	Malcolms	1
Joel Tapley	McCrareys	2
Richard Terry	Stephens	2
Joseph Turner	Whites	1
Jane Tompkins (widow)	Whites	1
William Tompkins' orphans	Whites	1
Elisha P. Turner	Whites	2
James C. Terondet	Malcolms	1
Hiram B. Troutman	McCrareys	2
Jared Tarpley	McCrareys	1
Isaac N. Troutman, orphan	McCrareys	1
John S. Thomas	Whites	1
Samuel Tucker	Husons	1
Esther Torrance (widow)	Malcolms	1
Andrew Torrance's orphans	Malcolms	1
Mansfield Torrance	Malcolms	1
Watkins Tapley	McCrareys	1
Mary Thomas (widow)	Whites	1
David Thomas' orphans	Whites	1
Eden Taylor	Stephens	2
Philip Trapp	Husons	1
Rachel Trapp (widow)	Husons	1

Applicant's Name and Remarks	Captain's District	Draws
Thomas Tinsley	Malcolms	1
Willis Trice	Husons	1
Vincent E. Vickers	Malcolms	1
Nancy Vickers (widow)	Malcolms	1
Elizabeth Virdin (widow)	Husons	1
Jane Virdin, orphan	Husons	1
John H. Ware	Malcolms	1
John Wootan	McCrareys	2
John Wise	McCrareys	2
Kissiah Willis, widow, whose husband died in the late war	McCrareys	2
minor orphans of Robert Willis, whose father died in the later war	McCrareys	2
Robert Willis, Junior	McCrareys	1
Britton Willis	McCrareys	2
Drury Wilkinson	Husons	1
Allen Watson	Husons	1
Hiram A. Wood	Husons	1
Louiza Weatherly, orphan, J. Cook, next friend	Husons	1
David Worsham's orphans	Stephens	1
David G. Worsham	Stephens	2
William White	Stephens	2
Rachel White (widow)	Stephens	1
John E. White	Stephens	2

Applicant's Name and Remarks	Captain's District	Draws
John Wallis	Stephens	1
Emanuel Wingate	Stephens	2
George S. Worsham	Stephens	1
Wiley Wicker	Stephens	1
Robert Watson	Stephens	1
Charlotte Wicker, orphan	Stephens	1
Jeremiah Worsham	Whites	2
John A. Wicker	Whites	1
Julius Wickers' orphans	Whites	1
~~Pryor Wright~~	Malcolms	~~2~~
Charlton Wright	Malcolms	2
Joseph Washburn	Husons	1
John G. Worsham	Stephens	2
Leroy M. Wiley	Malcolms	1
Amos Wingate	Husons	2
Elisha Whitney	Husons	1
John C. Walters	Husons	1
George White	Whites	1
William Wilson	McCrareys	1
Elizabeth Wall (widow)	Malcolms	1
James Wall's orphans	Malcolms	1
Ambrose Whittle	McCrareys	2

The foregoing was received & registered by James Fleming, R. D. L. L.

Major R. W. Ellis' Battalion

The following transcription is from the second item on the second roll of microfilm and consist of the applicants residing in five of the militia districts comprising Major Richard W. Ellis' Battalion. The list appears in the same original record volume, following the list for Major Young's Battalion.

On the first page, the clerk wrote the following.

Land Lottery

Georgia   } Names of persons Entitled to draw belonging to Richd W. Ellis^s Battalion of Baldwin County } S^d County enroll^d In this Book by H. Allen in 1821.

> *Capt Doziers District Number 317*
> *Capt Russels District Number 105*
> *Capt Doles District Number 318*
> *Capt Haws District Number*
> *Capt McGees District Number 319*

Names Person s intitled to Draw with Remarks in R. W. Ellis^s Battalion

The list is consists of a table with three columns, the first column containing the name of the applicant and any identifying remarks recorded by the clerk, the second column the militia district where the applicant resided, and the thrird column the total number of draws to which the applicant was entitled.

Immediately to the right of the name J. Shaw Ready, some placed a question mark, by whom, when, and for what purpose anyone's guess. In the margin, immediately to the left of the name of Luke Robertson, someone wrote the name Robinson, apparently correcting the entry, but again, by whom, when, and whether actually a correction, another quess.

Three entries for three applicants residing in Captain White's District appear on the following list, in spite of most others who appear on the previous list.

Applicants Name and Remarks	Captains District	Draws
[smudge] of Milledgeville	Traviller Journeymans	1
Anderson, Jones	Doles'	1
Anderson, Asa	Doles'	1
Allums, Nancy, a widow	Doles'	1
Allums, Bryant, Nancy Allums, John Allums, Betsey Allums, orphans of Asa Allums, dec^d	Doles'	1
Ailsey, James, house joiner	Haws	2
Anderson, Gideon	Doles	1
Atkins, Thomas, House Joiner	McGees	2
Anderson, Benjamin	McGees	1
Akridge, Ezekiel	McGees	1
Brooks, Charity, a widow	Doziers	1
Brooks, Martha, Gatsey Brooks, Mary Brooks, Elkanah Brooks, Elbert Brooks, Eliza Brooks, Semantha Brooks, orphans of Samuel Brooks, dec^d	Doziers	1
Wiley Brooks	Doziers	1
Butler, Charles, William Butler, Elizabeth Butler, orphans of Charles Butler, dec^d	McGees	1
Butler, Jonaes	McGees	1
Bass, Sterling, a farmer	Russels	2
Broadnax, Elizabeth, a widow	Russels	1
Blakely, Fountain S.	Russels	1

Applicants Name and Remarks	Captains District	Draws
Battson, David, a farmer	Russels	2
Battson, John Small	Russels	1
Butts, Lewis	Doziers	1
Boon, William, a farmer	Doles	1
Boynton, Amos F.	Russels	2
Bevins, Sarah, a widow	Russels	1
Bevins, Nancy, Appleton Bevins, Levena Bevins, Lotty Bevins, Cynthea Bevins, orphans of Jonathan Bevins, dec^d	Russels	1
Burges, William, orphan of Daniel Burges, dec^d	Doles	1
Bass, Martha, a widow	Doles	1
Beasley, William, a farmer	Doles	2
Butts, William R.	Doles	1
Bridges, James	Haws	2
Beasly, Stephen	Haws	1
Barnard, John	Haws	2
Bridges, Corben L.	Haws	2
Barrow, Lucy, a widow	McGees	1
Barrow, Haywood S., Lucazar C. Barrow, orphans off James Barrow, dec^d	McGees	1
Buckhannon, Sarah, a widow	McGees	1
Buckhannon, Thomas Jefferson, Robert Buckhannon, orphans of Robt Buckhannon, dec^d	McGees	1

Applicants Name and Remarks	Captains District	Draws
Boyington, Moses	McGees	2
Bevins, Shadrack	McGees	2
Boyington, John C.	McGees	1
Brown, Mark, fishing Creek	Doles	2
Barrington, John, fishing Creek	McGees	1
Babb, Elizabeth, a widow	Doles	1
Barksdale, Horatio	Doziers	1
Baker, Jean, a widow	McGees	1
Brown, Stephen	Doles	1
Brown, Edwards	Whites	1
Blount, Major	Doziers	1
Brown, Thomas C.	Whites	1
Barrett, Nancy & others, orphans of Isaac Barrett, dec[d]	Doles	1
Barker, Elizabeth, a widow	McGees	1
Barker, Edmund W.	McGees	1
Colbert, William B.	Doziers	1
Cook, Jeremiah	Doziers	1
Cole, Isaac, blacksmith	McGees	1
Cobb, Jacob, a farmer	Doziers	1
Coon, James, old soldier	Doziers	1
Curry, Thomas Jefferson, Samuel Adams Curry, Frederick William Curry, orphans of John C. Curry, dec[d]	Russels	1

Applicants Name and Remarks	Captains District	Draws
Crittendon, Robert G.	Doles	2
Clayton, Samuel	Haws	2
Cone, Joseph	Haws	2
Cone, Jackson	Haws	1
Cavennah, Catharine, a widow	McGees	1
Cavennah, Thomas, Polly Cavennah, John M. Cavenah, Edward Cavennah, Nancy Cavennah, Eliza M. Cavennah, orphans of George Cavennah, dec^d	McGees	1
Cooper, Davis	McGees	2
Cook, Burrell	Doziers	1
Clements, Stephen	Doles	2
Collins, James, a gin maker	Doles	1
Cousins, Greene, farmer, Capt	Doles	2
Collins, Robert	McGees	2
Collins, David	McGees	1
Collins, Moses	McGees	2
Cox, Turner	McGees	1
Collins, Aron	Doles	1
Calhoun, Susan V. Man, orphan of Irwin Calhoun, dec^d	Doziers	1
Calhoun, James S.	Doziers	1
Calhoun, Philip T.	Doziers	1
Chapman, Mary, orphan of Laban Chapman, dec^d	McGees	1

Applicants Name and Remarks	Captains District	Draws
Chapman, John D.	Stephens	2
Chapman, Mary, a widow	Stephens	2
Cooper, Jeremiah	McCrarys	2
Clark, John, Governor	McCrarys	2
Danielly, Sarah, a widow	Russels	1
Danielly, Mariah, Luezar Danielly, James Danielly, orphans of Arthur Danielly, dec^d	Russels	1
Danielly, Thomas	Russels	1
Dozier, Agness, a widow	Haws	1
Dismukes, Elizabeth, a widow	McGees	1
Dodds, John F., wagon maker	McGees	2
Daniel, William	McGees	2
Daniel, Young	McGees	1
Dunnivent, Daniel	Doles	2
Davidson, Fountin	Doles	1
Dorsey, Dennis William, orphan of Dennis Dorsey, dec^d	Doles	1
Doles, John	Doles	2
Doles, Zachariah, an orphan of Lemon Doles, dec^d	Doles	1
Doziers, James P., Capt	Doziers	2
Darden, William, orphan of Dempsey Darden, dec^d	McGees	1
Disharoon, John E.	Doziers	1

Applicants Name and Remarks	Captains District	Draws
Digby, Nathaniel	McGees	1
Dismukes, James	Doles	2
Dawson, Georgeena, orphan of John Dawson, dec^d	Doziers	1
Elliott, Mary, orphan of William Elliott, dec^d	Doziers	1
Ellis, Richard W., Maj^r	McGees	2
Evans, Elizabeth, a widow	Doziers	1
Evans, Mary, John Evans, Patsey Evans, orphans of John Evans, dec^d	Doziers	1
Ellis, William, M. G.	McGees	2
Ellis, John	McGees	2
Ellis, Austin	McGees	1
Evrett, Silas	Doziers	2
Freeny, John M., orphan of Robert Freeny, dec^d	Haws	1
Ford, Abraham	Doziers	2
Ford, Wiley W.		1
Fortner, Rowland	Doziers	2
Flewellen, Ann, a widow	Doles	1
Flewellen, Margarett, an orphan of Abner Flewellen, dec^d	Doles	1
Folys, James Henry	Husons	2
Fortner, Mary, a widow	Doziers	1
Gordy, Wilson	Roussels	1

Applicants Name and Remarks	Captains District	Draws
Gordy, William, Junr	Roussels	1
Greene, Miles, Junr, a farmer	Doziers	1
Gregory, Thomas	Doziers	1
Godwin, Kinchen William	Roussels	1
Greene, Robert, a farmer	Doles	2
Griggs, Timothy	Doles	1
Gholson, Eggleston	Haws	1
Grant, Priscilla, a widow	McGees	1
Grant, Charles, James Grant, John Grant, Anderson Grant, Greene Grant, Elizabeth Grant, orphans of Charles Grant, dec^d	McGees	1
Gill, Jesse	Doles	1
Gachett, Benjamin	Haws	2
Gill, Sherwood Small	Doles	1
Greene, John H.	Doziers	2
Gates, Thomas J.	McGees	1
Hubbard, John	Roussels	1
Hubbard, Thadeus	Roussels	1
Hendrick, John, a farmer	Doles	2
Harvey, William, Capt formerly	Doles	2
Hendrick, Mary, a widow	Doles	1
Haws, Claborn, Captain	Haws	2
Huff, Edward, a farmer	Haws	2
Ham, William, Melton Ham,	Haws	2

Applicants Name and Remarks	Captains District	Draws
Malinda Ham, Stephen Ham, John Ham, orphans of Bartell Ham, dec[d]		
Horton, Edmund, a farmer	Haws	2
Hudgins, Jane, a widow	McGees	1
Humphres, James, Esq[r]	Doles	2
Harp, Dixon, a farmer	McGees	2
Harp, John, a farmer	McGees	1
Hyatt, James, a tanner	Doles	2
Harvy, Maryann J., a widow	Haws	1
Harvy, Stephen	Doles	2
Howard, John, Jun[r]	Doles	2
Huff, William H.	Doles	1
Hill, James A.	McGees	2
Humphries, William C.	McGees	2
Hill, Elizabeth, a widow	McGees	1
Hill, Thomas, Louisa Hill, Amanda Hill, orphans of Robert H. Hill, dec[d]	McGees	1
Hill, Alexander L.	McGees	1
Hill, John	McGees	1
Harvy, Edward G.	Doziers	1
Hall, Clarkey, Mary Hall, Pool Hall, Burrell Hall, Aliza Hall, Nancy Hall, orphans of James Hall, dec[d]	McCrarys	1
Holt, Sarah, a widow	Doziers	1

Applicants Name and Remarks	Captains District	Draws
Hendrick, Obediah, Polly D. Hendrick, Elizabeth Hendrick, Benjamin Hendrick, Mastin D. Hendrick, orphans of John Hendrick, dec^d	Doles	1
Hughes, James	McCrarys	2
Hass, Henry	Doziers	2
Howard, John, Senr	Malcombs	2
Howard, Thacker B.	Malcombs	1
Howard, Homer V.	Malcombs	1
Harper, Mary, a widow	Malcombs	1
Adaline Harper, orphan of Solomon Harper, dec^d	Malcombs	1
Hughes, John	Malcombs	2
Horn, Elijah W.	McGees	1
Johnston, Gideon	Doziers	2
Jones, Edee, a widow	Doziers	1
Jones, Lucy, Eliza Jones, orphans of William Jones, dec^d	Doziers	1
Jackson, Thomas, a farmer	Doziers	1
Jones, Benjamin	Haws	1
Jones, Cooper	Haws	1
Jolley, Asa	McGees	1
Irby, James Jackson, orphan of James Irby, dec^d	Doles	1
Jackson, Sarah, a widow	Doles	1

Applicants Name and Remarks	Captains District	Draws
Jolley, James	McGees	2
Jolley, William	McGees	1
Jones, Ambrose	Russels	2
Jenkins, Walter S.	Stephens	2
John Johnston	Malcombs	1
King, James	Russels	1
King, John	Doles	2
Lewis, Fanny, a widow	Russels	1
Lewis, James Kannon, Elizabeth B. Lewis, Lucey A. Lewis, John E. Lewis, Robert S. Lewis, Charles F. Lewis, orphans of John Lewis, dec^d	Russels	1
Lord, Henry, a farmer	Russels	2
Lockett, Royall, saddler	Haws	2
Long, Nancy, a widow	McGees	1
Long, Polly, Charles Long, Elizabeth Long, Arthur Long, Lucinda Long, Susanna Long, orphans of Drury Long, dec^d	McGees	1
Leonard, Francis	McGees	1
Leonard, James C.	McGees	1
Lemley, Solomon D.	McCrarys	1
Lester, Benjamin P.	Doziers	1
Lester, William C.	Doziers	1
Lee, Thomas	McGees	2

Applicants Name and Remarks	Captains District	Draws
McGinty, William, a farmer	Russels	2
McGinty, Robert, Senr, a preacher	Russels	2
Moore, John, Senr	Russels	1
Moore, Whittington, blacksmith	Russels	1
Mitchell, William S., J. N.	Russels	1
Moore, Levinah, a widow	Russels	1
Mandevill, Charles G.	Haws	1
Morris, Joseph	Haws	1
Morris, James	Haws	2
Moore, Seabron, a Miller	Haws	1
Moore, Spencer, a farmer	Haws	2
Morris, Thomas	Haws	1
McKinney, William	McGees	1
McKinney, Grissom	McGees	1
Miles, John, Esqr	McGees	2
Miles, William, Junr	McGees	1
Moore, All Can, orphan of Luke Moore, dec^d	Doles	1
Martin, John L.	McGees	2
Meacham, Henry, Junr	Doles	1
Mercier, Benjamin P.	Doles	1
Meacham, Henry, Senr	Doles	2
McGinty, Meshack	Doles	2
Moses, Jean, Margaret Moses, Martha Moses, orphans of Saml	McGees	2

Applicants Name and Remarks	Captains District	Draws
Moses, dec[d] & mother dead also		
Moore, Mary, a widow	Doles	1
Miles, Aquilla	McGees	1
McGee, Jacob	McGees	1
Moore, Martha, Elizabeth Moore, Susan Moore, John Moore, Alfred Moore, Aromenta Moore, orphans of Morris Moore, dec[d]	Doles	1
McKinney, Jean, a widow	McGees	1
McKinney, John	McGees	1
Mathews, Josiah	Doles	2
Moughon, Thomas	Doziers	2
Musslewhite, Harriet, Musslewhite, Greene, orphans of Drury Musslewhite, dec[d]	Malcombs	1
Musslewhite, Thomas	Malcombs	1
Martin, Seabron, Jesse Martin, orphans of Cullen Martin, dec[d]	Doles	1
Malone, Charles, a preacher	Doziers	2
McDaniel, Daniel, orphan of Daniel McDaniel, dec[d]	Doziers	1
McDaniel, James	Doziers	1
Malone, John A.	Doziers	1
Norris, Robert	Doles	2
Nichols, Allen L.	McGees	2
Newsome, Anthony	Husons	1

Applicants Name and Remarks	Captains District	Draws
Pitts, Henrietta B., Payton T. Pitts, & Columbus A. Pitts, orphans of Jn° Pitts, dec^d	Russels	1
Pitts, Jack, a farmer	Russels	1
Parham, Robert	Russels	1
Parham, Mathew A.	Russels	1
Perry, Amos P., house joiner	Russels	1
Palmer, Christopher	Russels	1
Pickett, Elizabeth, a widow	Haws	1
Pickett, Richard, an orphan of Wm Pickett, dec^d	Haws	1
Perdue, George, a farmer	Haws	2
Persons, Josiah, a farmer	McGees	2
Palmer, Larkin	Doles	1
Parham, Benj. J., orphan of Stith Parham, dec^d	Haws	1
Psalter, Zabel	Haws	1
Pool, William W.	McGees	1
Page, James	Doles	1
Parker, Simeon	Doles	1
Perry, James	McCrarys	1
Page, Robbin	Doles	1
Potee, Ellender, a widow	Haws	1
Potee, Caroline E., Benjamin P. Potee, Joseph W. Potee, orphans of Benjamin Potee, dec^d	Haws	1

Applicants Name and Remarks	Captains District	Draws
Rogers, Polly, a widow	Doziers	1
Redding, James P. a farmer	Doziers	2
Redding, Rowland	Doziers	1
Roper, John M.	Doles	2
Redding, Parham D.	Haws	1
Rice, George W.	Haws	1
Reynolds, Robert, a farmer	Haws	2
Reynolds, James	Haws	2
Reed, Jeremiah	McGees	1
Ray, W. D.	Doles	2
Runnolds, William, a farmer	McGees	2
Ready, J. Shaw ?	McGees	2
Reynolds, Sarah, a widow	McGees	1
Reynolds, Mary, an orphan of Joshua Reynolds, dec^d	McGees	1
Rutherford, Benjamin H.	McGees	2
Robertson, Luke [in left margin Robinson]	Whites	1
Redding, Martha W., Haden Redding, Louiza H. Redding, Malinda Redding, & James F. Redding, orphans of Archer Redding. The last named orphan entitled to one sixth of one draw, the other five entitled to two, there Father & Mother being dead & last wife living yet.	Haws	2
Rogers, William B., a doctor	Husons	1

Applicants Name and Remarks	Captains District	Draws
Scott, John R., mechanic	Russels	2
Skinner, Florey, a widow	Russels	1
Skinner, Ebenezar, John Skinner, Isaac Alfred Skinner, Henry Skinner, Larkin Skinner, orphans of Henry Skinner, dec^d	Russels	1
Smith, John, a farmer	Doziers	1
Searcy, William	Doziers	2
Searcy, Aaron	Doziers	2
Scurlock, John	Doziers	1
Spikes, Andrew	Russels	1
Skinner, William, a farmer	Russels	1
Sawyer, Charles, a farmer	Doles	2
Sawyer, Zadock, a farmer	Doles	2
Smith, Mary, a widow	Doles	1
Spier, John M.	Haws	1
Stevens, John, Waters of Potatoe Creek	Haws	2
Simpson, George	McGees	2
Scurlock, Joshua	McGees	2
Sheppard, David	Doles	1
Simmons, Elijah	Haws	1
Sarell, John B.	Haws	2
Scroggin, William D., Esqr	Doles	1
Scrogin, James	Doles	1

Applicants Name and Remarks	Captains District	Draws
Scogin, Smith, Jun[r]	Doles	1
Spencer, Richard	McGees	1
Slaughter, John	McGees	2
Smallpiece, Thomas Andrew Jackson, orphan of Tho[s] Smallpiece, dec[d]	McGees	1
Sims, Judith, a widow	Doziers	1
Searcy, Benjamin R.	Haws	1
Tomlinson, James	Doles	1
Tansey, David	Doles	1
Tansey, Eli	Doles	1
Tomlinson, Mary, a widow	Doles	1
Tomlinson, Sarah, Benjamin C. Tomlinson, J. D. Maryann Tomlinson, orphans of John Tomlinson, dec[d]	Doles	1
Tickner, Orray, Doct[r]	Haws	2
Tapley, William	Haws	1
Trice, Patience, a widow	Doziers	1
Elisha Trice, Jean Trice, Patience Trice, Benjamin Trice, Thomas Jefferson Trice, James Madison Trice, Martha Ann Trice, Louiza L. Amanda M. Trice, orphans of Benjamin Trice, dec[d]	Doziers	1
Tiller, Bagwell B.	McGees	1
Tiller, Paul Han, orphan of Joseph Tiller, dec[d]	McGees	1

Applicants Name and Remarks	Captains District	Draws
Thompson, William H.	McGees	1
Turner, Asa A., Doctor	Doles	2
Thomas, Martin, Elizabeth Thomas, Emmaly Thomas, James Thomas, Jonathan Thomas, orphans of Jonathan Thomas, dec[d]	Haws	1
Veazey, Thomas, a farmer	Haws	2
Veazey, James	Haws	1
Womble, Mariah, orphan of Drury Womble	Doziers	1
Woodall, Jacob	Doziers	2
Woodall, Tempy, an idiott	Doziers	1
Watson, John, Sen[r]	Doles	2
Watson, John, Shff	Doles	1
Walton, Henry W.	Doles	1
Wiley, Ann, a widow	Doziers	1
Wiley, J. Eliza, Lard H. Wiley, John B. Wiley, Sarah Ann Wiley, orphans of Moses Wiley, dec[d]	Doziers	1
Wynn, Patsey, a widow	Doziers	1
Wynn, Gabriel, Charles R. Wynn, John Westley Wynn, Thomas Harrison Wynn, Sarah Hobbs Wynn, Shady Ann Mason Wynn, Robert Tarpley Wynn, Anderson Westmoreland Wynn, orphans of Robert Wynn, dec[d]	Doziers	1
Whitfield, Allums, an Idiot	Doles	1
Wheeler, Henry	Doles	1

Applicants Name and Remarks	Captains District	Draws
Wheeler, Francis A. B.	Doles	1
Watson, Robert T.	McCrarys	1
Wilson, Elizabeth, a widow	Doziers	1
Womble, Edmund	Doziers	2
Walker, Barshaba, a widow	Haws	1
Young, Marmaduke N.	Haws	1

Georgia } I Certify that this Book Contains a True List of all the Names of persons Baldwin County } entitled to & Sworn before me in said County as entitled to Draw in the present Contemplated land Lottery this 30th July 1821.

H. Allen, J. I. C.

Captains Companys in Major Amos Young^s Battalion

    Captain Husons District Number
    Captain Malcombs District Number 419
    Captain Stephens Number
    Captain McCrarys District Number
    Captain Whites District Number

3 or missing pages

Land Lottery

Georgia } Names of persons Entitled to draw belonging to Richd W. Ellis^s Battalion of Baldwin County } S^d County enroll^d In this Book by H. Allen in 1821.

        Capt Doziers District Number 317
        Capt Russels District Number 105
        Capt Doles District Number 318
        Capt Haws District Number
        Capt McGees District Number 319

Names Person s intitled to Draw with Remarks in R. W. Ellis^s Battalion

Applicants Name and Remarks	Captains District	Draws

Applicants Name and Remarks	Captains District	Draws
Brooks, Charity, a widow	Doziers	1
Brooks, Martha, Gatsey Brooks, Mary Brooks, Elkanah Brooks, Elbert Brooks, Eliza Brooks, Semantha Brooks, orphans of Samuel Brooks, dec^d	Doziers	1
Wiley Brooks	Doziers	1
Butler, Charles, William Butler, Elizabeth Butler, orphans of Charles Butler, dec^d	McGees	1
Butler, Janaes	McGees	1
Bass, Sterling, a farmer	Russels	2
Broadnax, Elizabeth, a widow	Russels	1
Blakely, Fountain S.	Russels	1
Battson, David, a farmer	Russels	2
Battson John Small	Russels	1
Butts, Lewis	Doziers	1
Boon, William, a farmer	Doles	1
Boynton, Amos F.	Russels	2
Bevins, Sarah, a widow	Russels	1
Bevins, Nancy, Appleton Bevins, Levena Bevins, Lotty Bevins, Cynthea Bevins, orphans of	Russels	1

Applicants Name and Remarks	Captains District	Draws
Jonathan Bevins, dec^d		
Burges, William, orphan of Daniel Burges, dec^d	Doles	1
Bass, Martha, a widow	Doles	1
Beasley, William, a farmer	Doles	2
Butts, William R.	Doles	1
Bridges, James	Haws	2
Beasly, Stephen	Haws	1
Barnard, John	Haws	2
Bridges, Corben L.	Haws	2
Barrow, Lucy, a widow	McGees	1
Barrow, Haywood S., Lucazar C. Barrow, orphans off James Barrow, dec^d	McGees	1
Buckhannon, Sarah, a widow	McGees	1
Buckhannon, Thomas Jefferson, Robert Buckhannon, orphans of Robt Buckhannon, dec^d	McGees	1
Boyington, Moses	McGees	2
Bevins, Shadrack	McGees	2
Boyington, John C.	McGees	1
Brown, Mark, fishing Creek	Doles	2
Barrington, John, fishing Creek	McGees	1
Babb, Elizabeth, a widow	Doles	1
Barksdale, Horatio	Doziers	1

Applicants Name and Remarks	Captains District	Draws
Baker, Jean, a widow	McGees	1
Brown, Stephen	Doles	1
Brown, Edwards	Whites	1
Blount, Major	Doziers	1
Brown, Thomas C.	Whites	1
Barrett, Nancy & others, orphans of Isaac Barrett, dec^d	Doles	1
Barker, Elizabeth, a widow	McGees	1
Barker, Edmund W.	McGees	1
Colbert, William B.	Doziers	1
Cook, Jeremiah	Doziers	1
Cole, Isaac, blacksmith	McGees	1
Cobb, Jacob, a farmer	Doziers	1
Coon, James, old soldier	Doziers	1
Curry, Thomas Jefferson, Samuel Adams Curry, Frederick William Curry, orphans of John C. Curry, dec^d	Russels	1
Crittendon, Robert G.	Doles	2
Clayton, Samuel	Haws	2
Cone, Joseph	Haws	2
Cone, Jackson	Haws	1
Cavennah, Catharine, a widow	McGees	1
Cavennah, Thomas, Polly Cavennah, John M. Cavenah, Edward Cavennah, Nancy Cavennah, Eliza M. Cavennah,	McGees	1

Applicants Name and Remarks	Captains District	Draws
orphans of George Cavennah, dec^d		
Cooper, Davis	McGees	2
Cook, Burrell	Doziers	1
Clements, Stephen	Doles	2
Collins, James, a gin maker	Doles	1
Cousins, Greene, farmer, Capt	Doles	2
Collins, Robert	McGees	2
Collins, David	McGees	1
Collins, Moses	McGees	2
Cox, Turner	McGees	1
Collins, Aron	Doles	1
Calhoun, Susan V. Man, orphan of Irwin Calhoun, dec^d	Doziers	1
Calhoun, James S.	Doziers	1
Calhoun, Philip T.	Doziers	1
Chapman, Mary, orphan of Laban Chapman, dec^d	McGees	1
Chapman, John D.	Stephens	2
Chapman, Mary, a widow	Stephens	2
Cooper, Jeremiah	McCrarys	2
Clark, John Governor	McCrarys	2
Danielly, Sarah, a widow	Russels	1
Danielly, Mariah, Luezar Danielly, James Danielly, orphans of Arthur Danielly, dec^d	Russels	1

Applicants Name and Remarks	Captains District	Draws
Danielly, Thomas	Russels	1
Dozier, Agness, a widow	Haws	1
Dismukes, Elizabeth, a widow	McGees	1
Dodds, John F., wagon maker	McGees	2
Daniel, William	McGees	2
Daniel, Young	McGees	1
Dunnivent, Daniel	Doles	2
Davidson, Fountin	Doles	1
Dorsey, Dennis William, orphan of Dennis Dorsey, dec^d	Doles	1
Doles, John	Doles	2
Doles, Zachariah, an orphan of Lemon Doles, dec^d	Doles	1
Doziers, James P., Capt	Doziers	2
Darden, William, orphan of Dempsey Darden, dec^d	McGees	1
Disharoon, John E.	Doziers	1
Digby, Nathaniel	McGees	1
Dismukes, James	Doles	2
Dawson, Georgeena, orphan of John Dawson, dec^d	Doziers	1
Elliott, Mary, orphan of William Elliott, dec^d	Doziers	1
Ellis, Richard W., Maj^r	McGees	2
Evans, Elizabeth, a widow	Doziers	1

Applicants Name and Remarks	Captains District	Draws
Evans, Mary, John Evans, Patsey Evans, orphans of John Evans, dec^d	Doziers	1
Ellis, William, M. G.	McGees	2
Ellis, John	McGees	2
Ellis, Austin	McGees	1
Evrett, Silas	Doziers	2
Freeny, John M., orphan of Robert Freeny, dec^d	Haws	1
Ford, Abraham	Doziers	2
Ford, Wiley W.		1
Fortner, Rowland	Doziers	2
Flewellen, Ann, a widow	Doles	1
Flewellen, Margarett, an orphan of Abner Flewellen, dec^d	Doles	1
Folys, James Henry	Husons	2
Fortner, Mary, a widow	Doziers	1
Gordy, Wilson	Roussels	1
Gordy, William, Junr	Roussels	1
Greene, Miles, Junr, a farmer	Doziers	1
Gregory, Thomas	Doziers	1
Godwin, Kinchen William	Roussels	1
Greene, Robert, a farmer	Doles	2
Griggs, Timothy	Doles	1
Gholson, Eggleston	Haws	1

Applicants Name and Remarks	Captains District	Draws
Grant, Priscilla, a widow	McGees	1
Grant, Charles, James Grant, John Grant, Anderson Grant, Greene Grant, Elizabeth Grant, orphans of Charles Grant, dec^d	McGees	1
Gill, Jesse	Doles	1
Gachett, Benjamin	Haws	2
Gill, Sherwood Small	Doles	1
Greene, John H.	Doziers	2
Gates, Thomas S.	McGees	1
Hubbard, John	Roussels	1
Hubbard, Thadeus	Roussels	1
Hendrick, John, a farmer	Doles	2
Harvey, William, Capt formerly	Doles	2
Hendrick, Mary, a widow	Doles	1
Haws, Claborn, Captain	Haws	2
Huff, Edward, a farmer	Haws	2
Ham, William, Melton Ham, Malinda Ham, Stephen Ham, John Ham, orphans of Bartell Ham, dec^d	Haws	2
Horton, Edmund, a farmer	Haws	2
Hudgins, Jane, a widow	McGees	1
Humphres, James, Esqr	Doles	2
Harp, Dixon, a farmer	McGees	2
Harp, John, a farmer	McGees	1

Applicants Name and Remarks	Captains District	Draws
Hyatt, James, a tanner	Doles	2
Harvy, Maryann J., a widow	Haws	1
Harvy, Stephen	Doles	2
Howard, John, Jun[r]	Doles	2
Huff, William H.	Doles	1
Hill, James A.	McGees	2
Humphries, William C.	McGees	2
Hill, Elizabeth, a widow	McGees	1
Hill, Thomas, Louisa Hill, Amanda Hill, orphans of Robert H. Hill, dec[d]	McGees	1
Hill, Alexander L.	McGees	1
Hill, John	McGees	1
Harvy, Edward G.	Doziers	1
Hall, Clarkey, Mary Hall, Pool Hall, Burrell Hall, Aliza Hall, Nancy Hall, orphans of James Hall, dec[d]	McCrarys	1
Holt, Sarah, a widow	Doziers	1
Hendrick, Obediah, Polly D. Hendrick, Elizabeth Hendrick, Benjamin Hendrick, Mastin D. Hendrick, orphans of John Hendrick, dec[d]	Doles	1
Hughes, James	McCrarys	2
Hass, Henry	Doziers	2
Howard, John, Sen[r]	Malcombs	2

Applicants Name and Remarks	Captains District	Draws
Howard, Thacker B.	Malcombs	1
Howard, Homer V.	Malcombs	1
Harper, Mary, a widow	Malcombs	1
Adaline Harper, orphan of Solomon Harper, dec^d	Malcombs	1
Hughes, John	Malcombs	2
Horn, Elijah W.	McGees	1
Johnston, Gideon	Doziers	2
Jones, Edee, a widow	Doziers	1
Jones, Lucy, Eliza Jones, orphans of William Jones, dec^d	Doziers	1
Jackson, Thomas, a farmer	Doziers	1
Jones, Benjamin	Haws	1
Jones, Cooper	Haws	1
Jolley, Asa	McGees	1
Irby, James Jackson, orphan of James Irby, dec^d	Doles	1
Jackson, Sarah, a widow	Doles	1
Jolley, James	McGees	2
Jolley, William	McGees	1
Jones, Ambrose	Russels	2
Jenkins, Walter S.	Stephens	2
John Johnston	Malcombs	1
King, James	Russels	1
King, John	Doles	2

Applicants Name and Remarks	Captains District	Draws
Lewis, Fanny, a widow	Russels	1
Lewis, James Kannon, Elizabeth B. Lewis, Lucey A. Lewis, John E. Lewis, Robert S. Lewis, Charles F. Lewis, orphans of John Lewis, dec[d]	Russels	1
Lord, Henry, a farmer	Russels	2
Lockett, Royall, saddler	Haws	2
Long, Nancy, a widow	McGees	1
Long, Arthur, Long, Lucinda, Long, Susanna, Long, orphans of Drury Long, dec[d]	McGees	1
Leonard, Francis	McGees	1
Leonard, James C.	McGees	1
Lemley, Solomon D.	McCrarys	1
Lester, Benjamin P.	Doziers	1
Lester, William C.	Doziers	1
Lee, Thomas	McGees	2
McGinty, William, a farmer	Russels	2
McGinty, Robert, Sen[r], a preacher	Russels	2
Moore, John, Sen[r]	Russels	1
Moore, Whittington, blacksmith	Russels	1
Mitchell, William S., J. N.	Russels	1
Moore, Levina, a widow	Russels	1
Mandevill, Charles G.	Haws	1
Morris, Joseph	Haws	1

Applicants Name and Remarks	Captains District	Draws
Morris, James	Haws	2
Moore, Seabron, a miller	Haws	1
Moore, Spencer, a farmer	Haws	2
Morris, Thomas	Haws	1
McKinney, William	McGees	1
McKinney, Grissom	McGees	1
Miles, John, Esqr	McGees	2
Miles, William, Junr	McGees	1
Moore, All Can, orphan of Lie Moore, dec^d	Doles	1
Martin, John L.	McGees	2
Meacham, Henry, Jun	Doles	1
Mercier, Benjamin P.	Doles	1
Meacham, Henry, Sen	Doles	2
McGinty, Meshack	Doles	2
Moses, Jean, Margaret Moses, Martha Moses, orphans of Saml Moses, dec^d & mother dead also	McGees	2
Moore, Mary, a widow	Doles	1
Miles, Aquilla	McGees	1
McGee, Jacob	McGees	1
Moore, Martha, Elizabeth Moore, Susan Moore, John Moore, Alfred Moore, Aromenta Moore, orphans of Morris Moore, dec^d	Doles	1
McKinney, Jean, a widow	McGees	1

Applicants Name and Remarks	Captains District	Draws
McKinney, John	McGees	1
Mathews, Josiah	Doles	2
Moughon, Thomas	Doziers	2
Musslewhite, Harriet, Musslewhite, Greene, orphans of Drury Musslewhite, dec^d	Malcombs	1
Musslewhite, Thomas	Malcombs	1
Martin, Seabron, Jesse Martin, orphans of Cullen Martin, dec^d	Doles	1
Malone, Charles, a preacher	Doziers	2
McDaniel, Daniel, orphan of Daniel McDaniel, dec^d	Doziers	1
McDaniel, James	Doziers	1
Malone, John A.	Doziers	1
Norris, Robert	Doles	2
Nichols, Allen L.	McGees	2
Newsome, Anthony	Husons	1
Pitts, Henrietta B., Payton T. Pitts, & Columbus A. Pitts, orphans of Jno Pitts, dec^d	Russels	1
Pitts, Jack, a farmer	Russels	1
Parham, Robert	Russels	1
Parham, Mathew A.	Russels	1
Perry, Amos P., house joiner	Russels	1
Palmer, Christopher	Russels	1
Pickett, Elizabeth, a widow	Haws	1

Applicants Name and Remarks	Captains District	Draws
Pickett, Richard, an orphan of Wm Pickett, dec^d	Haws	1
Perdue, George, a farmer	Haws	2
Persons, Josiah, a farmer	McGees	2
Palmer, Larkin	Doles	1
Parham, Benj. J., orphan of Stith Parham, dec^d	Haws	1
Psalter, Zabel	Haws	1
Pool, William W.	McGees	1
Page, James	Doles	1
Parker, Simeon	Doles	1
Perry, James	McCrarys	1
Page, Robbin	Doles	1
Potee, Ellender, a widow	Haws	1
Potee, Caroline E., Benjamin P. Potee, Joseph W. Potee, orphans of Benjamin Potee, dec^d	Haws	1
Rogers, Polly, a widow	Doziers	1
Redding, James P. a farmer	Doziers	2
Redding, Rowland	Doziers	1
Roper, John M.	Doles	2
Redding, Parham D.	Haws	1
Rice, George W.	Haws	1
Reynolds, Robert, a farmer	Haws	2
Reynolds, James	Haws	2

Applicants Name and Remarks	Captains District	Draws
Reed, Jeremiah	McGees	1
Ray, W. D.	Doles	2
Runnolds, William, a farmer	McGees	2
Ready, J. Shaw ?	McGees	2
Reynolds, Sarah, a widow	McGees	1
Reynolds, Mary, an orphan of Joshua Reynolds, dec^d	McGees	1
Rutherford, Benjamin H.	McGees	2
Robertson, Luke [in left margin Atkinson]	Whites	1
Redding, Martha W., Haden Redding, Louiza H. Redding, Malinda Redding, & James F. Redding, orphans of Archer Redding. The last named orphan entitled to one sixth of one draw, the other five entitled to two, there Father & Mother being dead & last wife living yet.	Haws	2
Rogers, William B., a doctor	Husons	1
Scott, John R., mechanic	Russels	2
Skinner, Florey, a widow	Russels	1
Skinner, Ebenezar, John Skinner, Isaac Alfred Skinner, Henry Skinner, Larkin Skinner, orphans of Henry Skinner, dec^d	Russels	1
Smith, John, a farmer	Doziers	1
Searcy, William	Doziers	2
Searcy, Aaron	Doziers	2

Applicants Name and Remarks	Captains District	Draws
Scurlock, John	Doziers	1
Spikes, Andrew	Russels	1
Skinner, William, a farmer	Russels	1
Sawyer, Charles, a farmer	Doles	2
Sawyer, Zadock, a farmer	Doles	2
Smith, Mary, a widow	Doles	1
Spier, John M.	Haws	1
Stevens, John, Waters of Potatoe Creek	Haws	2
Simpson, George	McGees	2
Scurlock, Joshua	McGees	2
Sheppard, David	Doles	1
Simmons, Elijah	Haws	1
Sarell, John B.	Haws	2
Scroggin, William D., Esq[r]	Doles	1
Scrogin, James	Doles	1
Scogin, Smith, Jun[r]	Doles	1
Spencer, Richard	McGees	1
Slaughter, John	McGees	2
Smallpiece, Thomas Andrew Jackson, orphan of Tho[s] Smallpiece, dec[d]	McGees	1
Sims, Judith, a widow	Doziers	1
Searcy, Benjamin R.	Haws	1
Tomlinson, James	Doles	1

Applicants Name and Remarks	Captains District	Draws
Tansey, David	Doles	1
Tansey, Eli	Doles	1
Tomlinson, Mary, a widow	Doles	1
Tomlinson, Sarah, Benjamin C. Tomlinson, J. D. Maryann Tomlinson, orphans of John Tomlinson, dec^d	Doles	1
Tickner, Orray, doct^r	Haws	2
Tapley, William	Haws	1
Trice, Patience, a widow	Doziers	1
Elisha Trice, Jean Trice, Patience Trice, Benjamin Trice, Thomas Jefferson Trice, James Madison Trice, Martha Ann Trice, Louiza L. Amanda M. Trice, orphans of Benjamin Trice, dec^d	Doziers	1
Tiller, Bagwell B.	McGees	1
Tiller, Paul Han, orphan of Joseph Tiller, dec^d	McGees	1
Thompson, William H.	McGees	1
Turner, Asa A., doctor	Doles	2
Thomas, Martin, Elizabeth Thomas, Emmaly Thomas, James Thomas, Jonathan Thomas, orphans of Jonathan Thomas, dec^d	Haws	1
Veazey, Thomas, a farmer	Haws	2
Veazey, James	Haws	1
Womble, Mariah, orphan of Drury Womble	Doziers	1

Applicants Name and Remarks	Captains District	Draws
Woodall, Jacob	Doziers	2
Woodall, Tempy, an idiott	Doziers	1
Watson, John, Sen[r]	Doles	2
Watson, John, shff	Doles	1
Walton, Henry W.	Doles	1
Wiley, Ann, a widow	Doziers	1
Wiley, J. Eliza, Lard H. Wiley, John B. Wiley, Sarah Ann Wiley, orphans of Moses Wiley, dec[d]	Doziers	1
Wynn, Patsey, a widow	Doziers	1
Wynn, Gabriel, Charles R. Wynn, John Westley Wynn, Thomas Harrison Wynn, Sarah Hobbs Wynn, Shady Ann Mason Wynn, Robert Tarpley Wynn, Anderson Westmoreland Wynn, orphans of Robert Wynn, dec[d]	Doziers	1
Whitfield, Allums, an idiot	Doles	1
Wheeler, Henry	Doles	1
Wheeler, Francis A. B.	Doles	1
Watson, Robert T.	McCrarys	1
Wilson, Elizabeth, a widow	Doziers	1
Womble, Edmund	Doziers	2
Walker, Barshaba, a widow	Haws	1
Young, Marmaduke N.	Haws	1

Georgia } I Certify that this Book Contains a True List of all the Names of persons Baldwin County } entitled to & Sworn before me in said County as entitled to Draw in the present Contemplated land Lottery this 30th July 1821.

H. Allen, J. I. C.

Captains Companys in Major Amos Young^s Battalion

        Captain Husons District Number
        Captain Malcombs District Number 419
        Captain Stephens Number
        Captain McCrarys District Number
        Captain Whites District Number

Taliaferros
Milledgeville District
Lafferty
(older than the two preceeding books)

[smudge] Littleton	1						1
Allen, Harris	2						2
Allen, John	2						2
Ayers, William	1						1
Austin, John	1						1
Akridge, John	1						1
Akridge, Abel	2						2
Allen, Couzie		1					1
Blithe, F. Anne				1			1
Bird, Thompson	2						2
Bird, John G.	1						1
Bridggers, James C.	1						1

Boon, John	2							2
Betts, Elisha	2							2
Brown, John U.	2							2
Britton, Harriet		1						1
Britton, Harriot for orphans of John Britton					1			1
Boon, William	1							1
Brown, Phebe		1						1
Brown, Phebe for orphans of William Brown					1			1
Betton, Solomon	1							1
Brown, Samuel							1	1
Boorin, Joseph	2							2
Buchannan, H. L. Reverend	1							1
Ball, William	2							2
Bozeman, John	2							2
Barrow, James, Senr	1							1
Bevin, William	2							2
Bevin, William for the orphans of Shadrack Bevin					1			1
Brown, William	2							2
Burgy, Henry	2							2
Bower, Benannuel	1							1
Burden, Elizabeth		1						1
Baxter, Thomas W.	2							2

Barrow, Jacob	2						2
Barrow, Jacob for orphans of Moses Barrow				1			1
Betton, Charles F. M.	1						1
Brady, Nathan, Jun	1						1
Bowles, David	1						1
Bevin, William	1						1
Bradford, Thomas M.	1						1
Berry, James	1						1
Beckum, Absalon B.	1						1
Bulger, Daniel	2						2
Bush, Henry	1						1
Bowers, Arthur	2						2
Bozeman, James	2						2
Barrow, William	1						1
~~Brown, Thomas C.~~	1						1
~~Babb, William~~	2						2
Bostwick, Anne		1					1
Bostwicke, Anne for orphans of Chesley Bostwick				1			1
Buffington, Samuel	2						2
Blackshear, Bryan	1						1
Banister, Kersey	1						1
Boykin, Samuel	2						2
Bowen, William	1						1

Barkley, James	2						2
Brown, John F.	2						2
Brown, Thomas C.	1						1
Brown, Edards	2						2
Boykin, James	2						2
Babb, William	2						2
Brown, Mildred		1					1
Brown, Mildred for orphans of John Brown, dec^d				1			1
Bevin, John	1						1
Borland, William	2						2
Calhoun, James S.	1						1
Cook, Benjamin	2						2
Crow, Thomas S.	2						2
Cooper, John M.	2						1	3
Cook, Joseph	2						2
Collier, John	2						2
Cumbest, John	2						2
Clements, Thomas	1						1
Christian, Charles	2						2
Clark, William B.	2				2		4
Cooper, William	1						1
Collier, Richard	2						2
Cline, Abram	2						2

Covey, James	1								1
Cary, Edward	2								2
Cone, Samuel	2								2
Coleman, Sophiah		1							1
Coleman, Sophiah for orphans of Elliot Coleman					1				1
Craft, Hugh	1								1
Cook, Isaac	2								2
Crenshaw, William H.	2								2
Covey, John	2								2
Christian, Elijah W.	1								1
Chapman, Berry S.	1								1
Chambliss, William	1								1
Callaway, John	2								2
Callaway, Jacob	1								1
Callaway, John	2								2
Chapman, Isaiah	2								2
Chandler, Sarah		1							1
Chandler, Sarah for orphans of Danl Chandler					1				1
Doster, Joshua	1						2		3
Doster, Malachi	1								1
Dannelly, William J.	1								1
Davis, William	1								1
Dannelly, Arthur S.	1								1

Dannelly, Thomas	2						2
Dyer, Eliphalet C.	1						1
Doud, Amasa	1						1
Dunnivant, Abel	1						1
Darnel, Henry for orphans of Jo^{sh} Steele				1			1
Dickson, Thomas	2						2
Doyle, Dennis	2						2
Deracan, Hiram M.	2						2
Dubose, John	1						1
Dubose, Elias	1						1
Dubose, Peter	2				2		4
Everett, Silas	2						2
Easter, John C.	2						2
Elliott, Andrew	2						2
Ellington, Elizabeth		1					1
~~Eugene, William J.~~						1	1
Easter, Mary		1					1
Edwards, William L.	2						2
Eilands, Nancy		1					1
Eilands, Nancy for orphans of Isaiah Eilands				1			1
Ferrell, Salley		1					1
Ferrell, Bryant, orphan				1			1
~~Fair, Peter~~					~~1~~		~~1~~

Finn, Greenberry	1					1
Felps, Robert A.	1					1
Fort, Zachariah C.	1					1
Fleming, James	2					2
Fleming, Laird	1					1
Francisco, John	1					1
Fort, Tomlinson	1					1
Freeman, Martha		1				1
Freeman, Martha for orphans of Fred Freeman				1		1
Freeney, William B.	1					1
Freeman, Joseph	1					1
Freeney, Rebecah		1				1
Freeney, Rebecah for orphans of Gillah Freeney				1		1
Franklin, Esom D.	2					2
Franklin, Esom D. for orphans of David Triplett				1		1
Franklin, Sampson	1					1
Freeman, William	2					2
Freeman, William for orphans of John Freeman				1		1
Freeman, Friend	1					1
Green, John	1					1
Gray, Priscilla		1				1
Griffin, John	1					1

Gent, Peter	2							2
Goodall, Samuel	2							2
Greene, Rodham A.	1							1
Gates, Thomas J.	1							1
Groves, John	1							1
Gamble, James	2							2
Glenn, James	1							1
Griggs, Rhodom S.	1							1
Griggs, Leroy P.	1							1
Glover, Mark	1							1
Glass, Nancy for orphans of John McKean					1			1
Goodwin, Mathew	2							2
Goolsby, Samuel	1							1
Greene, William	2							1
Griffin, William	1						2	3
Garner, Reddick	2							2
Goode, James	1							1
Griggs, Thomas	1							1
Greenlee, Samuel	1							1
Godwin, Simeon M.	1							1
Holt, Thaddeus G.	1							1
Holt, Thaddeus G. for the orphans of Thaddeus Holt								1
(to wit) Caroline S. & Fowler Holt					1			1

Holcombe, Henry B.	2							2
Harper, Mary		1						1
Harper, Mary for the orphans of Solomon Harper					1			1
Harrison,, James	1							1
Holt, Anderson	1							1
Howel, Sarah for the orphans of Daniel Howel					1			1
Huckaby, Brittain	2							2
~~Hammond, Abner~~	~~2~~							~~2~~ Jr
Harris, Drury						1		1
Holt, Milton	1							1
Hussar, Felix	1							1
Hood, William	1							1
Hammond, Daniel	2							2
Humphrey, Hardy P.	2							2
Howard, Edy		1						1
Howard, John, Senr	2							2
Howard, John H.	2							2
Hargrove, Laban	1							1
Hughes, Anna		1						1
Haas, Henry, of Capt Doziers District	2							2
Haas, Henry for orphans of John Dawson					1			1

Haas, Henry for orphans of Dan[1] McDaniel					1			1
Harper, Mary		1						1
Hodges, Abel	2							2
Hicks, John H.	2							2
Huchinson, William	2							2
Hicks, Sarah		1						1
Hoy, Clinton	2							2
Hicks, Daniel	2							2
Jones, Walter	2							2
Jones, Seaborn	2							2
Jones, Ezra B.	1							1
~~Jones, Joseph~~ Jones, Ezra B. for orphans of Joseph Jones	1				1			1
Jordan, Overoff	2					2		4
Jordan, Hezekiah by his father Overoff Jordan	2							2
Jeter, Francis	2							2
Jarrett, Patterson	2							2
Jarrett, William D.	2							2
Jarrett, Patterson for orphans of Devereaux Jarrett					1			1
Jarrett, Rebecah		1						1
Jones, Frances		1						1
Johnston, John	1							1

Jowell, Ratcliff	1							1
Jenkins, Polley W.		1						1
Jailett, Peter F.	2							2
Jones, John A. for orphans of Fleming Grantland					1			1
John A. Jones for Eliza Grantland A.		1						1
Jowell, Richard	2						2	4
Johnston, Nicholas	1							1
Johnston, Samuel	2							2
Jones, Gabriel	2							2
Jones, John	1							1
Jones, William	1							1
Johnston, Sarah		1						1
[smudge] Mildred S.					1			1
Knight, Thomas	1							1
King, George W.	2							2
King, George W. for orphans of James Howard					1			1
Kramer, David	2							2
Kenan, Thomas H. for orphans of Nathan Powell					1			1
Kirkpatrick, James	1							1
Kilpatrick, David	2							2
King, Hannah		1						1
King, Hannah for orphans					1			1

of Levi King							
Kraatz, John	2						2
Lucas, John	1						1
Lewis, William	2						2
Lewis, Fauntleroy	1						1
Lane, Edmund for orphans of Thos D. Clark					1		1
Logan, Philip	2					2	4
Logan, Joel	1						1
Logan, Philip for orphans of Hugh Logan					1		1
Langford, Edmund	2						2
Langford, Edmund for orphans of John Burden					1		1
Lacruse, Francis	2						2
Locke, Abner, Guardian for Elizabeth & Obedience Lowe, orphans of O. Lowe, dec^d					1		1
Locke, Abner, Guardian for Washington Dawson, orphan of John Dawson					1		1
Locke, Abner	1						1
Locke, Mary		1					1
Locke, Mary for Jesse Locke, orphan of Jonathan Locke					1		1
Lindsey, William	1						1
Lunsford, Rolen	1						1

Lucas, John, merch[t]	2						2
Lucas, Kezia		1					1
Lucas, John for orphans of James Lucas					1		1
Lenos, Charles	2						2
Lewis, Elizabeth		1					1
Lewis, William for orphan of Jn° Lewis					1		1
[smudge] William, agent for Augustus Lewis of Hancock County of Captain Mims District	2						2
Lee, Salley		1					1
Leonard, Benjamin	2						2
Leonard, Joseph	1						1
Lacey, John B.	1						1
Leonard, John	2						2
[faint]	2						2
Lee, Salley for orphans of John McLee of Marshalls District					1		1
McGehee, George					1		1
Morgan, Richard M.	1						1
Malone, Henry W.	1						1
Moss, James	1						1
Moss, Epps	1						1
Moncrief, Sterling	1						1

McCarty, Cornelius	2							2
Micklejohn, Robert	1							1
Musclewhite, William	1							1
Murphy, Daniel	2							2
Murphy, Ellis	1							1
Murphy, Drury	1							1
Meadows, Miles	1							1
Marsh, Hesther		1						1
Marsh, Hesther for orphans of Eli Marsh					1			1
McMillan, Daniel	1							1
Meacham, James	1							1
McGehee, Samuel	1							1
Moore, Bartholomew B.	1							1
Malone, Charles	2							2
Martin, William	1							1
McCoy, Alexander	1							1
Marcus, Thomas	2							2
Murden, Mildred		1						1
Murden, Mildred for orphan of Jeremiah Murden					1			1
Mitchell, John	1							1
Moffit, Gabriel C.	1							1
McDaniel, Samuel	1							1
Mitchell, John	1							1

Marshall, James	1						1
Molpus, Jeremiah	2					2	4
Montgomery, James	2						2
Montgomery, James for orphans of Berry Patillo					1		1
Minor, Mary		1					1
Minor, Mary for orphans of John B. Minor					1		1
Moran, John	2						2
Moran, William	2						2
Moran, Jesse	1						1
Moran, Frances		1					1
Moran, Frances for orphan of Elisha Moran					1		1
Morris, Obediah	2						2
Morris, Obediah for orphan of Ephraim Moore					1		1
Martin, Ailey		1					1
Martin Ailey for orphans of David Martin					1		1
Martin, William	1						1
Miller, Nathaniel	2						2
Miller, Nathaniel for orphan of Joseph T. Slade					1		1
Nipper, William	1						1
Neeley, Richard	1						1
Newsom, Anthony	1						1

Orme, Richard M.	1							1
Owens, Anne		1						1
O'Daniel, Alexander	1							1
Pike, Polley		1						1
Pike, Polley for orphans of Nathaniel Pike					1			1
Pierce, Lovick, Sen	2							2
Pelham, Edward	1							1
Preswood, Robert	2							2
Pulliam, William	1							1
Porter, Samuel	2							2
Perry, Willis	1							1
Proctor, Martha R.		1						1
Paschal, Dennis	1							1
Parr, James	1							1
Philips, Benjamin							1	1
Pryor, Marlow	2							2
Pace, David	1							1
Pulley, Benjamin	2							2
Pride, John	2							2
Robertson, William	2							2
Richards, Christopher C.	1							1
Rutherford, Robert	2							2
Redding, William C.	1							1
Rucker, Mary Anne		1						1

Rucker, Mary Anne for orphan of George Rucker					1			1
Rowe, Chauncey	1							1
Rucker, Jane for orphans of Willis Rucker					1			1
Raford, Patience		1						1
Rousseau, James	2							2
Ray, William	1							1
Ratclif, George	1							1
Reid, John	1							1
Reid, William	2							2
Reid, Templeton	1							1
Rona, Joseph	1							1
Robinson, Solomon	2							2
Robinson, Luke	1							1
Robinson, William	1							1
Robinson, John R.						1		1
Stubbs, Thomas B.	2							2
Sanders, Stephen	2							2
Sturges, Daniel	2							2
[faint] Joseph [faint]				1	1			2
Stovall, Joseph	2							2
Sanford, Frederick	2							2
Stephens, Simeon L.	1							1
Stanford, James	2							2

~~Swan, Salley~~		0					0
~~Salley Swan for orphan of Ebenezer Swan~~					0		0 Jr
Stubbs, Baradell P.	1						1
Spencer, Alonson	2						2
Salter, Richard	1						1
Stone, Michael	2						2
Scurlock, Daniel	1						1
Sims, Benjamin	1						1
Stubbs, Peter	1						1
Stoughtenburg, Peter B.	1						1
Sturges, Benjamin H.	1						1
Simpson, John	2						2
Stone, William D.	2						2
Shackleford, Edmund	2						2
Smith, John	1						1
Sanford, Jess of [blank] District	2						2
Summerton, Thomas	2						2
Steeley, James	2						2
Smith, John R.	2						2
Simpson, George	2						2
Smith, James	1						1
Smith, Sarah		1					1
Slaughter, Daniel	2						2

Trapp, Thomas	2						2
Terondet, James C.	1						1
Trapp, Phillip	1						1
Thornton, Henry	2						2
Trapp, Thomas Guardian for Joseph Sims orphan				1			1
Thomas, George	1						1
Tulley, John A.	1						1
Turner, Joshua	2						2
Tucker, Joseph	2						2
Turner, Milborn	1						1
Taylor, Martha		1					1
Taylor, Martha for orphans of William Taylor				1			1
Taliaferro, Richard C.	2						2
Thomas, David	2						2
Thomas Sherrod	1						1
Tompkins, Jane		1					1
Tompkins, Jane for orphans of Wm Tompkins				1			1
Vickers, Vincent E.	1						1
Vickers, Nancy		1					1
Vass, John M.	2						2
Williams, Anderson	2						2
Weeks, William	1						1
Ware, John H.	1						1

Williams, John	1							1
Wall, Eliza	1	1						1
Washington, Robert B.	2							2
Washington, Robert B., Junr	1							1
Watson, Robert	1							1
Watson, Caty		1						1
Weatherly, William	2							2
Willey, Leroy M.	1							1
Willey, Leroy M. for orphans of Moses Wiley					1			1
Whitaker, Simon	2							2
Winget, Amos	2							2
Watson, Allen	1							1
Wilson, James	2							2
Ware, William W.	1							1
Wright, Charlton	1							1
Watson, Alexander, Junr	1							1
Wright, Pryor	2							2
Wright, John H.	2							2
Wiseman, John	2							2
Whallis, Francis	2							2
Wright, William	1							1
Wood, Elisha	1							1
Willis, William	1							1

Woodall, Archibald	2							2
Williamson, Charles	2							2
Williamson, Eugene J.							1	1
Wooten, John for orphans of Joseph Selby					1		1	2
Winget, Richard B.	2							2
Worsham, Jeremiah	2							2
Winget, Michael	2							2
Welch, William	2							2
Winget, Emmanuel	1							1
Wheeler, David	2							2
Willowby, John	1							1
John A. Jones								
Hughes, James Irwins District 2 draws								
Ogden, Solomon captain Irwins District 4 draws								
R. Rutherford 122								
Geo. W. King 76								
Trapp 25								
Smith, Sarah Taliaferro District 1 draw widow								

Index

Elizabeth, 140
John, 96
Abbott
  Eli, 126
Ailsey
  James, 146
Akridge
  Abel, 36, 59
  Ezekiel, 82, 146
  John, 36, 59
  Joseph E., 82, 126
  William, 82, 94
  William B., 126
Allen
  Cousie, 36, 59
  Cuzza, 126
  H., 145, 163
  Harris, 36, 59, 94
  John, 36, 59, 126
Allums
  Asa, 146
  Betsey, 146
  Bryant, 146
  John, 11, 94, 146
  Nancy, 146
  Whitfieald, 11
Anders
  Joseph, 11, 94
  Stephen R., 11
Anderson
  Abijah, 82, 94
  Asa, 146
  Benjamin, 146
  Gideon, 11, 146
  James, 11
  Jones, 146
Andrews
  William J., 126
Appleby
  Henrey, 11
Armstrong
  Laborn, 126
  Wiley, 126
Ashton
  Nathaniel, 94
Askew
  James L., 126
Atkerson
  John, Sr., 94
Atkins
  Thomas, 146
Atkinson
  Littleton, 36, 59, 94
Austin
  John, 36, 59, 94
Ayers
  Abraham, 126
  William, 36, 59, 126
Babb
  Elizabeth, 12, 148
  William, 38, 61, 95
Bailey
  Henry, 82
Baker
  Janes, 12
  Jean, 148
  Jeremiah, 12
Ball
  William, 37, 60, 126
Banister
  Henry, 38, 61
Barker
  Edmund W., 148
  Elizabeth, 148
Barkley
  James, 38, 61, 96, 97
Barksdale
  Horatio, 148
  Terrell, 96
Barksdell
  Terrell, 13
Barnard
  John, 13, 147
Barnes
  Maxy, 128
Barrentine
  Jacob, 12, 94, 96

John, 11
Barrett
  Isaac, 148
  Nancy, 148
Barrew
  Lucy, 11
Barrington
  John, 148
Barron
  Jacob, 94
  Joseph, 37, 60
Barrow
  Haywood S., 147
  Henry, 82, 97
  Jacob, 37, 60
  James, 11, 147
  James, Jr., 126
  James, Sr., 37, 60, 126
  Lucazar C., 147
  Lucy, 147
  Moses, 37, 60
  William, 38, 61, 96
Bartow
  Henry, 95
Bass
  Martha, 12, 147
  Sterling, 12, 146
Bateman
  James, 82, 127
Battson
  David, 147
  John Small, 147
Baxter
  Thomas W., 37, 60, 97
Beal
  Tanday, 12
Bealle
  Tandy, 97
Beasley
  Charles, 82
  John J., 12
  William, 147
Beasly
  Stephen, 147
  William, 12
Beckam
  Absalom B., 37, 60
Beckham
  Absalom B., 95
  Albert G., 128
  Allen, 95
  Labun, 96
Beckhannan
  Green B., 11
Beckum
  Allen, 82
  Laban, 82
Bedingfield
  John, 128
Belding
  William, 128
Bell
  M. R., 32
Benning
  Thomas C., 127
Berry
  James, 37, 60, 127
Betton
  Charles F. M., 37, 60
  Solomon, 37, 60, 128
Betts
  Elisha, 36, 59, 95, 97
Bevin
  John, 39, 62, 96
  Milley, 83
  Shadrack, 37, 60
  William, 37, 60
Bevins
  Appleton, 147
  Cynthea, 147
  James, 95
  Jonathan, 147
  Levena, 147
  Lotty, 147
  Nancy, 147
  Sarah, 147
  Shadrack, 148
  Thomas, 82
Bickers
  John, 83
Bird
  John C., 36, 59

John G., 128
Thompson, 36, 59, 97
Bivins
  James, 11
  John, 11
  Milley, 126
  Rolen, 127
  Shadrach, 126
  Shedrick, 11
  Thomas, 127
  William, 127
Blackshear
  Bryan, 38, 61
Blair
  Robert, 95
Blakely
  Fountain S., 146
Blakey
  David, 12, 96
Blithe
  J. Anne, 36, 59
Blount
  Major, 148
Bodnax
  Elizabeth R., 12
Boler
  Joel, 96
  John, 96
  Nancy, 95
Boon
  John, 36, 59, 95
  William, 36, 59, 147
Booren
  Joseph, 97
Boothe
  Benagah, 128
  Leroy, 128
Boren
  William, 96
Borland
  William, 39, 62, 96
Bostick
  Ann, 128
  Chesley, 128
Bostwick
  Anne, 38, 61

  Chesley, 38, 61
  Joshua, 95
Bowen
  Joseph, 95
  William, 38, 61, 94
Bower
  Benanuel, 127
  Bennannuel, 60
  Bennanuel, 37
Bowers
  Arthur, 38, 61
  Benjamin, 82, 126
  Jesse, 82, 95
Bowles
  David, 37, 60
  David W., 128
Box
  Lemmons, 127
  Mary, 127
  Maty, 82
  Shadrach, 82, 127
Boyington
  John C., 148
  Moses, 148
Boykin
  James, 38, 61, 127
  Samuel, 38, 61, 96
Boynton
  Amos F., 147
  Moses, 12
Bozeman
  Chloe, 127
  James, 38, 61, 96, 97
  James N., 127
  John, 37, 60, 96
Braddy
  Nathan, 95
  Nathan, Jr., 33, 37
Bradford
  Thomas M., 37, 60, 95
Brady
  Nathan, Jr., 33, 60
Branham
  Thomas, 83, 96
Brantley
  Edmund, 11, 96

Braser
  Henrey, 12
Bressie
  William, 126
Brewer
  Henry, 95, 97
Bridgers
  James C., 95
Bridges
  Corben L., 147
  James, 13, 147
  Reuben, 13
Bridggers
  James C., 36, 59
Britain
  Tilman, 92
Britt
  Obed, 82, 97
Britton
  Harriet, 36, 59, 97
  John, 36, 59, 95
Brksdell
  John, 13
Broadnax
  Elizabeth, 146
Brooks
  Charity, 146
  Elbert, 146
  Eliza, 146
  Elkanah, 146
  Gatsey, 146
  Hiram, 127
  Ivey, 96
  Ivy, 82
  John Z., 82, 127
  Martha, 146
  Mary, 146
  Maxey, 82, 95
  Samuel, 12, 96, 146
  Semantha, 146
  Simon, 82, 97
  Wiley, 146
Brown
  Drewcillar, 127
  Edwards, 38, 61, 148
  Elizabeth, 127
  Hollinger, 11
  John, 38, 61
  John F., 38, 61, 95, 97
  John M., 95
  John U., 36, 59
  Joseph, 23
  Loam, 126
  Manassa, 127
  Mark, 11, 148
  Mark M., 83
  Mathew, 11
  Mildred, 38, 61, 95
  Phebe, 36, 59, 97
  Richard G., 127
  Robert, 126
  Samuel, 37, 60, 127
  Stephen, 148
  Stephen A., 12
  Thomas C., 38, 61, 148
  Uriah, 127
  William, 12, 36, 37, 59, 60, 126
  William P., 83, 96
  William, Sr., 128
Browning
  Rowanna E., 128
  Sarah F., 128
Bruen
  Timothy, 128
Bryant
  James, 127
Buchanan, 4
  Robert, 11
Buchannan
  H. L. Revinus, 37, 60
  Revinus H. L., 95
Buckhanan
  Sarah, 11
Buckhannon
  Robert, 147
  Robt., 147
  Sarah, 147
  Thomas Jefferson, 147
Buffington
  Samuel, 38, 61, 96
Bulger
  Daniel, 38, 61, 95

Burch
  John, 9, 127
Burden
  Elizabeth, 37, 60
  John, 47, 70
Burges
  Daniel, 147
  William, 147
Burgess
  Samuel, 82, 126
Burgy
  Henry, 37, 60
Burnside
  James, 12
Burt
  Robert, 13
Bush
  Henry, 38, 61
Butler
  Charles, 146
  Elizabeth, 146
  Jonaes, 146
  William, 146
Butts
  Lewis, 12, 147
  Wednesday, 32
  William R., 147
Byington
  Amos F., 12
Calaway
  John, 128
Calhoon
  Elbert, 15, 99
  Michael, 15
  Phillip, 15
Calhoun
  Irwin, 149
  James F., 39
  James S., 62, 149
  Philip T., 149
  Susan V. Man, 149
Callaway
  Elijah, 13
  Elisha, 13, 129
  Jacob, 40, 63, 100
  John, 40, 63, 129

  Levin, 13, 99
  Sarah, 14, 129
Camak
  James, 128
Candler
  Daniel, 129
  William L., 129
Carey
  Edward, 97
Carter
  John T., 129
  Mary, 84, 99
  Thomas, 84
Cary
  Edward, 39, 62
Castleberry
  Thomas, 97
Castlebury
  Thomas, 83
Cavenah
  George, 13, 98, 99
  John M., 149
Cavennah
  Catherine, 149
  Edward, 149
  Nancy, 149
  Polly, 149
  Thomas, 149
Cay
  John, 128
  William, 84, 128
Chambliss
  Alexander, 83
  Edmd., 99
  John, 83, 98
  William, 40, 63
  Zachariah, 83, 99
Chancellor
  John, 84
  William, 84
Chandler
  Danl., 40, 63
  Sarah, 40, 63
Chapman
  Ambroes, 14
  Berry S., 40, 63, 98

Isaiah, 40, 63, 99
John D., 83, 150
Laban, 14, 149
Mary, 83, 149, 150
Chappell
  Henry, 129
  Samuel, 129
Chesher
  William, 98
Cheshers
  Turpin, 99
Christian, 40
  Charles, 39, 62, 99
  Elijah W., 63
Clark
  John, 8, 14, 84, 122, 129, 150
  Thos. D., 47, 70
  William B., 39, 62, 128
Clarke
  Alfred, 14, 98
Clayton
  Samuel, 149
Clem
  Henrey, 14
Clements
  Mathew, 83, 100
  Matthew, 98
  Stephen, 14, 149
  Thomas, 15, 39, 62
Cline
  Abram, 39, 62, 129
Cloud
  Reubin, 129
Clower
  Thomas, 14, 98
Cobb
  Benjamin, 83, 128
  Darling, 83, 129
  Jacob, 128, 148
  Joseph, 83, 129
  Joseph, Sr., 83
  Levi, 14, 97
  Mark, 83, 129
Cochram
  Thomas, 15
Cochran

  Thomas, 100
Cocks
  Polley, 129
Colbert
  William, 84
  William B,, 148
Cole
  Isaac, 148
Coleman
  Elliot, 39, 62
  Sarah, 98
  Sophia, 39
  Sophiah, 39, 62
  Willis, 99
Collier
  John, 39, 62, 98
  Richard, 39, 62, 98, 99
Collins
  Aaron, 13
  Andrew, 31, 98
  Aron, 149
  David, 149
  Dennis, 97, 99
  James, 14, 98, 99, 149
  Joseph, 14, 98
  Moses, 13, 149
  Robert, 13, 149
Colman
  Sarah, 13
  Thomas, 13
  William, 13
  Willis, 14
Colvin
  Daniel, 129
Cone
  Bazzel, 99
  Brazzel, 15
  Jackson, 149
  James, 14, 98
  John, 15, 100
  Joseph, 15, 149
  Samuel, 39, 62
Coney
  Andrew, 128
Cook
  Arthur B., 13

Arthur, Jr., 97
Benjamin, 39, 62
Burrell, 149
Henry, 13, 98
Isaac, 39, 62
J., 143
Jeremiah, 148
Joseph, 39, 62, 98
Philip, 129
William, 15, 100
Coon
  James, 148
Cooper
  Davis, 13, 149
  Edmund, 23, 99
  Jeremiah, 150
  John M., 39, 62
  Thomas, 13, 98
  William, 39, 62, 99
Copland
  Isaac, 128
Corey
  John, 40, 63
Corry
  James, 39, 62
Cousins, 4, 10
  Green, 14
  Greene, 149
Covey
  James, 130
  John, 98
Cox
  Henry, 83, 130
  John, 88, 98
  Turner, 149
  Willis, 83, 98, 99
  Zilpha, 83, 129
Crabtree
  John, 83
Craft
  Hugh, 39, 62, 100
Crawford
  Joel, 129
Crenshaw
  William H., 39, 62
  Wm. H., 99

Crittenden
  Robert G., 14
Crittendon
  Robert G., 149
Crow
  Thomas S., 39, 62, 99
Crowder
  Bushrod, 129
  Hiram, 129
  John M., 84, 99
Cumbest
  John, 39, 62, 97
Cumming
  Robert R., 129
Cunningham
  Samuel, 14, 98, 99
Currie
  John C., 14
  John H., 14
  Sarah, 14, 99
Curry
  Cary, 13, 98, 99
  Elisha, 14, 99
  Frederick William, 148
  John C., 148
  Samuel Adams, 148
  Thomas Jefferson, 148
Cushing
  Elisha, 130
  Isaac T., 129
Dadd
  Isaac, 84, 100
Danelly
  Arthur, 130
  William J., 130
Danely
  Arthur, 16
Daniel
  William, 15, 150
  William J., 33, 40
  Young, 15, 150
Danielly
  Arthur, 150
  James, 150
  Luezar, 150
  Mariah, 150

Sarah, 150
Thomas, 150
Dannelly
  Arthur S., 40, 63
  Thomas, 40, 63
  William J., 33, 63
Darbey
  James, 16
Darby
  John, 131
Darden
  Dempsey, 150
  William, 150
Darnel
  Henry, 40, 63
Daud
  Amasa, 33, 40
Davanne
  John P., 130
Davice
  Esaw, 15
  Hugh, 16
  William, 15, 100
Davidson
  Fountain, 150
Davis
  Arthur B., 130
  Cross R., 130
  Esau, 130
  Jesse, 130
  John, 84, 100
  Mary, 130
  Thomas, 15, 96, 101
  Timothy, 101
  Toliver, 84, 100
  William, 40, 63
Dawson
  Fountain, 15
  Georgeena, 151
  John, 34, 44, 47, 67, 70, 151
  Washington, 34, 47, 70, 101
Dean
  James, 130
  Jane, 130
  William, 130
Dees

John, 130
Densler
  Henry, 16
Densley
  Henry, 100
Dent
  Samuel, 21
Dentz
  Samuel, 100
Deracan
  Hiram M., 41, 64, 100, 101
Dickson
  Thomas, 40, 63, 100
  William, 130
Digby
  Joseph, 84, 131
  Nathaniel, 84, 151
  William, 100
Disharoon
  John E., 150
Dismuck
  Betsy, 15
  John, 100
Dismucks
  John, 15
Dismukes
  Elizabeth, 150
  James, 151
Dodds
  John F., 150
Doles, 4, 145
  Benjamin, 4, 16, 100, 101
  Jesse, 16, 100, 101
  John, 150
  Lemon, 16, 150
  Zachariah, 150
Dorsey
  Denis, 15
  Dennis, 150
  Dennis William, 150
  Jackey, 15
  Jackey B., 100
Dortic
  George T., 130
Doster
  Joshua, 40, 63, 101

Malachi, 40, 63, 101
Doud
  Amasa, 33, 63, 101
Douglass
  Jones, 84, 100
Downer
  John, 16, 100
Doyle
  Dennis, 41, 64, 100
Dozier, 4, 44, 67, 145
  Agnes, 16
  Agness, 150
  James P., 16
  Jane, 4
Doziers
  James P., 150
Driver
  John, 84
Dubose
  Elias, 41, 64
  John, 41, 64
  Peter, 41, 64
  Peter, Sr., 130
Duffy
  Owen, 130
Dunivent
  Daniel, 15
Dunnivant
  Abel, 33
Dunnivent
  Daniel, 150
Durby
  James, 100
Dyer
  Eliphalet, 130
  Eliphalet C., 40, 63
  Thomas, 130
Easter
  John C., 41, 64, 101
  Mary, 41, 64, 131
Edge
  John, 84
Edwards
  William, 16, 101
  William B., 131
  William L., 41, 64, 131

Eilands
  Isaiah, 41, 64, 101
  Nancy, 41, 64, 131
Ellington
  Elizabeth, 41, 64, 101
Elliott
  Andrew, 41, 64, 101
  Mary, 151
  William, 151
Ellis, 4, 10
  Austin, 16, 151
  Fielding, 16, 101
  John, 151
  R. W., 125
  Richard W., 16, 151
  Richd. W., 145
  Thomas M., 16, 101
  William, 16, 151
Estes
  Allen, 131
Ethridge
  Caleb, 84, 101
  John, 131
  Marmaduke, 84, 101
Eugene
  William J., 41, 64
Evans
  Elizabeth, 16, 151
  John, 17, 151
  Mary, 151
  Nancy, 131
  Patsey, 151
  Thomas, 17, 101
  Turner, 16
Everett
  Silas, 41, 64
Evrett
  Silas, 151
Fair
  Peter, 41, 64
Felps
  Robert A., 41, 64
Ferell
  Mary Ann B., 132
  Sarah A., 132
Ferrell

Bryant, 41, 64
Salley, 41, 64
Few
  Ignatius, 131
  Lenidas, 131
Fields
  Thompson, 17, 102
Finn
  Greenberry, 41, 64
Flake
  John P., 17
Fleming
  James, 41, 64, 144
  John, 131
  Laird, 42, 65, 131
Flemming
  James, 102
Fletcher
  Joseph, 84
Flewellen
  Abner, 17, 151
  Ann, 17, 151
  Margaret, 17, 151
Foard
  Wyatt, 131
Folys
  James Henry, 151
Ford
  Abraham, 151
  Francis, 17
  Wiley W., 151
Fort
  Tomlinson, 42, 65, 131
  Zachariah C., 41, 64
Fortner
  Mary, 151
  Rowland, 151
Francisco
  John, 42, 65, 131
Franklin
  Esam D., 131
  Esom D., 42, 65
  Sampson, 42, 65
  Simpson, 131
Freeman
  Fred, 42, 65

Frederick, 131
Friend, 42, 65
  John, 42, 65, 101
  Joseph, 42, 65, 131
  Martha, 42, 65
  William, 42, 65, 131
Freeney
  Elijah, 17
  Gillah, 42, 65
  Rebecah, 42, 65
  Robert, 20
  William B., 42, 65
Freeny
  Elijah, 102
  Gillah, 102
  John M., 151
  Robert, 151
  William B., 102
French
  Charles H., 131
Fuller
  John, 84, 102
  Jones, 17, 102
Gachet
  Benjamin, 18
Gachett
  Benjamin, 152
Gafford
  Hannah, 85, 102
  John, 85, 102
  Thomas, 85, 103
Gailord
  Giles, 85
Gamble
  James, 43, 66, 132
Ganday
  Bretian, 21
  Britain, 102
Gardener
  Elias F., 132
Gardiner
  L., 83
Gardner
  Elias, 18
Garner
  Reddick, 43, 66, 103

Gaster
  James, 103
Gates
  Thomas J., 43, 66, 152
Gault
  John Henry, 17, 102
Gent
  Peter, 42, 65, 102
Gente
  Peter, 103
Gholson
  Eggleston, 152
Gilbert
  Josiah, 85
Gill
  Jesse, 17, 152
  Sherwood Small, 152
  William, 17, 103
Glass
  Nancy, 43, 66
Gleen
  James, 102
Glenn
  James, 43, 66
Glover
  Mark, 43, 66, 103
Godwin
  James, 18, 102
  Kinchen William, 152
  Simeon, 66, 132
  Simeon M., 43
  William F., 18
Golden
  Abraham, 132
  Isaac, 132
  John R., 132
Good
  James S., 132
  Samuel G., 132
Goodall
  Samuel, 42, 65, 103
Goode
  James, 43, 66
Goodwin
  Mathew, 43, 66
Goolsby
  Samuel, 43, 66
Gordon
  John P., 132
Gordy
  William, Jr., 152
  Wilson, 151
Gorman
  John, 132
Goslin
  Barnet, 18, 103
  James, 18, 102
Graham
  Archibald, 132
Grant
  Anderson, 152
  Charles, 152
  Elizabeth, 152
  James, 152
  John, 152
  Joseph, 17
  Priscilla, 17, 152
Grantland
  Eliza, 46, 69
  Eliza A., 132
  Fleming, 46, 69, 132
  Seaton, 132
Gray
  Priscilla, 42, 65, 102
Green
  John H., 18
  Raleigh, 102
  Raligh, 18
  Rodham A., 33
  William, 102
Greene
  Amos, 85, 102
  Benjamin, 85, 102
  Henry, 102
  John, 42, 65
  John H., 152
  Miles, 152
  Myles, 18, 103
  Rhodam A., 43
  Rhodom A., 132
  Richard, 85
  Richard A., 66

Robert, 152
Sarah, 132
Susan T., 132
William, 43, 66
William L., 132
Greenlee
  Samuel, 43, 66
Gregory
  Gregory, 152
Griffin
  Andrew, 85, 103
  John, 42, 65, 103
  William, 43, 66
Grigg
  William, 85, 103
Griggs
  John, 18
  Leroy P., 43, 66
  Rhodom S., 43, 66, 103
  Thomas, 43, 66, 102
  Timothy, 152
Grooms
  Wright, 132
Groves
  John, 43, 66
Guerry
  Theodore, 85, 102
Haas
  George, 134
  Henry, 44, 67
Haley
  John, 134
Hall
  Aliza, 153
  Burrell, 153
  Clarkey, 153
  James, 153
  Mary, 153
  Nancy, 153
  Pool, 153
Ham
  Bartell, 152
  Bartlett, 20
  John, 152
  Malinda, 152
  Melton, 152
  Stephen, 152
  William, 152
Hamet
  John, 104
Hammet
  John, 27
Hammond
  Abner, 44, 67, 86, 104
  Daniel, 44, 67, 104
Haney
  William, 103
Hargrove
  Jesse, 133
  Laban, 44, 67, 133
Harp
  Dixon, 18, 153
  John, 153
Harper
  Adaline, 154
  Mary, 44, 45, 67, 154
  Solomon, 44, 67, 154
Harris
  Allbas W., 133
  Drury, 44, 67
  Ellen G. C., 134
  Ezekiel, 20, 104, 105
  Mary, 85
  Sarah, 85
  Thomas, 85, 133
Harrison
  David, 86, 103
  Eli W., 133
  James, 44, 67
Harriss
  Elias, 133
Harvey
  John H., 86, 133
  Micael, 19
  Michael, 104
  Rachel, 18
  Rebecca, 19, 104
  Stephen, 19
  William, 18, 152
Harvill
  Samuel, 133
Harvy

Edward G., 153
Maryann J., 153
Stephen, 153
Harwell
  Sarah, 85, 104
  William, 85
Hass
  Henry, 154
Hawkins
  William, 18
Haws, 4, 10, 145
  Clabourn, 19
  Claburn, 152
  Claiburn, 4
  Newton, 19
Hendrick
  Benjamin, 154
  Elizabeth, 154
  Gustavus, 19
  Gustuvus, 104
  John, 19, 152, 154
  Mary, 152
  Mastin D., 154
  Obediah, 154
  Polly D., 154
Hendricks
  John, 104
Herring
  Charlotte, 86
  George, 86, 104
Hicks
  Daniel, 45, 68, 133
  John H., 45, 68, 104
  Sarah, 45, 68, 104
Higgans
  Thomas, 134
Hightower, 4
  Pleasant, 104
  Pleasant R., 19
  William, 104
Hill
  Alexander L., 153
  Amanda, 153
  David B., 85, 133
  Eli S., 103
  Elizabeth, 153

James A., 18, 153
John, 153
Judeath, 19
Judith, 104
Louisa, 153
Robert, 85, 133
Robert H., 18, 153
Thomas, 133, 153
Thos., 19
William, 133
Hines
  Abner, 19, 103, 104
  John B., 133
Hodges
  Abel, 45, 68, 133
Hodnett
  William, 18
Hogan
  Isham, 104
Holcolmbe
  Larkin, 134
Holcombe
  Henry B., 44, 67, 133
Hollingsworth
  William, 133
Holt
  Alfred B., 19
  Anderson, 134
  Caroline S., 43, 66
  Fowler, 43, 66
  Milton, 44, 67
  Sarah, 19, 153
  Thaddeus, 43, 66
  Thaddeus C., 43, 66
  Thaddeus G., 105
Hood
  William, 44, 67
Horn
  Elijah W., 154
  James, 18, 104
  William, 18, 103
Horton
  Edmund, 20, 153
  Stephen, 21, 104
House
  William G., 133

Howard
  Eadeth, 133
  Edy, 33, 44
  Homer V., 154
  James, 46, 69, 133
  John, 85
  John H., 44, 67, 105
  John, Jr., 153
  John, Sr., 33, 44, 154
  Thacker B., 154
Howel
  Daniel, 44, 67, 104
  Sarah, 44, 67
  William, 19
Howell
  Daniel, 105
  William, 104
Hoy
  Clinton, 45, 68
  William, 86, 103, 132
  William, Jr., 86
Hubbard
  John, 19, 152
  Mannoah, 103
  Manoah, 19, 103, 104
  Thadeus, 152
Huchinson
  William, 45, 68, 133
Huckabay
  Brittan, 103
Huckaby
  Brittain, 44, 67, 103
Hudgins
  Jane, 153
Huff
  Edward, 19, 152
  Travace, 19
  William H., 19, 153
Hughes
  Anna, 44, 67, 105
  James, 58, 86, 154
  John, 154
Humphres
  James, 153
  Thomas J., 19
Humphrey

Hardy P., 44, 67, 133
Humphries
  Thomas, 104
  William C., 153
Humpres
  James C., 19
Hunt
  Henry, 105
Huson, 4, 125, 163
  Marcus D., 132
  Thomas, 133
Hussar
  Felix, 44, 67
Hyatt
  James, 153
Irby
  James, 154
  James Jackson, 21, 154
Irvin
  George, 135
Irwin, 4, 33, 93
  James, 86
Ivey
  Barna, 134
  Robert, 134
  Turna, 134
Jackson
  Green B., 134
  Jacob, 20, 106
  Luke, 134
  Sarah, 20, 154
  Susannah, 20, 106
  Thomas, 20, 154
Jailett
  Peter F., 46, 69
Jaillet
  Peter F., 135
James
  Abel, 88
Jarrat
  Rebecca, 137
Jarratt
  Devereaux, 134
  Peterson, 135
  Rebecca F., 134
  William D., 106

Jarrett
  Devereaux, 45, 68
  Patterson, 45, 68
  Rebecah, 45, 68
  William D., 45, 68
Jeane
  Green, 106
  Greene, 20
Jenkins
  Benjamin, 21, 105
  Polley W., 46, 69, 105
  Walter S., 155
Jeter
  Fr., 93
  Francis, 45, 68, 135
  James A., 135
Jewell
  Mark M. R., 134
Johnson
  Samuel, 20
  Sarah, 134
Johnston
  Caleb, 86
  Gideon, 20, 154
  John, 46, 68, 155
  Loid, 20
  Loyd, 105
  Nicholas, 46, 69
  Samuel, 46, 69, 105
  Sarah, 46, 69, 106
  William, 20, 105
Joiner
  Absalom, 86
  Joseph, 86
  Mary, 86
Jolley
  Asa, 154
  James, 155
  William, 155
Jolly
  Asa, 20
  James, 20
  John, 20, 105
Jones
  Ambrose, 155
  Benjamin, 154
  Cannon, 135
  Cooper, 154
  Edee, 154
  Eliza, 154
  Ezra B., 45, 68, 134
  Frances, 45, 68, 106
  Francis, 86
  Gabriel, 46, 69, 106
  Henry L., 105
  James, 134
  John, 46, 69, 134
  John A., 21, 46, 58, 69, 106
  John W., 20, 106
  Joseph, 45, 68
  Joseph B., 105
  L. Henry, 20
  Lucy, 154
  Seaborn, 45, 68, 106
  Thomas B., 105
  Walter, 45, 68, 105
  William, 46, 69, 154
Jordan
  Hezekiah, 33, 45, 68, 105
  Mathew J., 134
  O., 33, 45
  Overoff, 33, 45, 68, 106
  William B., 86, 106
Jourdan
  Hezekiah, 105
Jowell
  Ratcliff, 46, 68
  Richard, 46, 69, 106
Joyner
  Absolam, 134
  Joseph, 134
  Mary, 134
Justice
  Dempsey, 86, 105
  Levi, 86, 105
Kemp
  Simeon, 21, 107
Kenan
  Hardy H., 135
  Lewis H., 135
  Thomas H., 34, 46, 69
Kennington

John, 135
Kennon
  William, 87, 106, 107
Ketler
  Mildred, 34, 46, 106
  Mildred S., 34, 69
Kilpatrick
  David, 47, 70, 106
  Richard, 21
Kimbrell
  Peter W., 135
Kimbrough
  Leonard, 135
King
  Geo. W., 58
  George W., 46, 69, 106, 133
  Hannah, 47, 70
  Howell, 125, 135
  James, 155
  John, 21, 155
  Levi, 47, 70
Kinglet
  Maryann, 106
Kirkpatrick
  James, 47, 69
  Thomas J., 135
Knight
  Robert, 106
  Thomas, 46, 69, 106
Kraatz
  Elizabeth, 135
  John, 34, 47, 69, 107, 135
Kramer
  David, 46, 69, 107
Lacey, 4
  John B., 48, 71
Lacruse
  Francis, 47, 70, 107
Lacy
  Philemon, 21
Ladd
  Jesse, 135
Lafield
  John, 21
Lamar
  C. Q. Lucius, 34, 48

Lucius Q. C., 108
Lane
  Edmund, 47, 70
Langford
  Edmund, 47, 70
Lankford
  Edmund, 135
Lassiter
  Robert, 136
Lawson
  John H., 21, 107
Ledbetter
  Henry, 22
  Sarah, 22
  William, 22
Lee
  Archibald, 135
  Salley, 48, 71
  Sarah, 136
  Thomas, 86, 155
Lemley
  Solomon D., 155
Lenos
  Charles, 48, 71, 107
Leonard
  Benjamin, 48, 71, 107
  Francis, 21, 155
  James C., 21, 155
  John, 48, 71, 136
  Joseph, 48, 71, 135
  Michael, 108
Lester
  Benjamin P., 155
  Hiram, 22, 108
  Isaac, 107, 108
  Isaac, Jr., 22
  Isaac, Sr., 22
  James, Sr., 22, 107
  John, 22, 107
  Julius, 108
  Wade, 22, 107
  William C., 22, 155
Lesueur
  Drury M., 86, 107
  Harrison, 136
  Jordon B., 135

Lewis
  Augustin, 48, 71
  Charles F., 155
  Elizabeth, 48, 71, 136
  Elizabeth B., 155
  Fanny, 155
  Fauntleroy, 47, 70
  Fielding, 136
  James Kannon, 155
  Jno., 48, 71
  John, 155
  John E., 155
  John T., 87, 135
  Lucey A., 155
  Robert S., 155
  Ulysses, 135
  William, 47, 48, 70, 71, 107
Lindsey
  William, 48, 71, 135
Lingo
  Richard T., 136
Lingold
  William, 136
Little
  Abraham, 108
  Allen, 22, 107
  John, 23, 107, 108
Locke
  Abner, 34, 47, 70, 136
  Jesse, 34, 47, 70, 136
  Jonathan, 34, 47, 70
  Mary, 34, 47, 70, 136
Lockett
  Royall, 155
Logan
  Hugh, 47, 70, 107
  Joel, 34, 70
  Philip, 34, 47, 70
  Phillip, 107, 108
Long
  Arthur, 155
  Charles, 155
  Drury, 21, 155
  Elizabeth, 155
  Evans, 86
  Lucinda, 155
  Nancy, 21, 155
  Nimrod W., 86, 108
  Polly, 155
  Susanna, 155
Lord
  Henry, 155
Loving
  Joseph S., 136
Low
  Edmund, 22, 107
Lowe
  Elizabeth, 34, 47, 70
  O., 34, 47, 70
  Obadiah, 136
  Obediance, 87, 136
  Obedience, 34, 47, 70
Lucas
  James, 48, 71
  John, 47, 48, 70, 71, 107
  Kezia, 48, 71, 107
Lumpkin
  Thomas, 136
Lunsford
  Rolen, 48, 71, 107
Lyman
  Daniel, 136
Maclin
  Edward, 110
  John, 110
  William J., 136
Maddox
  Abigail, 87
  Abigal, 138
  Benjamin, 87
  Joseph, 137
Mager
  Zacheus, 138
Malcolm, 4, 125
  John, 137
Malcomb, 163
Mallet
  James, 23
  Randol, 23
Malone
  Charles, 49, 72, 157
  Henry W., 48, 71, 137

John A., 157
Mandevill
  Charles G., 156
Mann
  Hiram, 138
Marchman
  John, 24, 109
Marcus
  Mary, 22
  Thomas, 49, 72, 101, 108, 110
Markey
  Patrick, 108
Marsh
  Eli, 49, 72, 138
  Hesther, 49, 72, 109
Marshall, 33, 48, 93
  James, 50, 73
Martain
  Alay, 138
  David, 138
  William, 137
Martin
  Ailey, 50, 73
  Benjamin, 24, 109
  Cullen, 157
  David, 50, 73
  Edmund, 87
  Jesse, 157
  John, 88
  John L., 23, 156
  Morris, 88, 108, 111
  Seabron, 157
  William, 49, 50, 72, 73
  Wm., 109
Massengale
  Reddick, 138
Massias
  Abram A., 139
Mathews
  Abraham, 23
  Josiah, 23, 157
Maxcy
  David A., 87
  Henry Thomas, 87
  Nathaniel, 87
Maxey

  David A., 110
  Thomas H., 110
Maynor
  Jesse, 137
McCarty
  Cornelius, 49, 72, 108
McClowd
  Hugh, 24
McColours
  Rachel, 139
McComack
  Catren, 87
McCoy
  Alexander, 49, 72
McCrarey, 4, 125
  Bartley, Jr., 137
  Bartley, Sr., 137
  Isaac, 139
  James, 4, 136
  Jonathan, 137, 138
  Robert, 136
  William, 137
McCrary, 163
  Bartley, Jr., 88, 109, 111
  Bartley, Sr., 88
  Hannah, 88, 89, 108
  Isaac, 87
  James, 88
  John, 87, 110
  Jon., 88
  Jonathan, 85
  Mathew, 88, 111
  Robert, 22, 88, 109
  Willie, 88, 109
McCullen
  Rachel, 87
McDaniel
  Daniel, 67, 157
  Danl., 44
  James, 157
  Samuel, 50, 73
McDonald
  Archibald, 23, 110
  Samuel, 110
McDonold
  Absalom, 87

McGee, 145
  Jacob, 157
McGehee, 4
  Edward, 22
  George, 48, 71
  James, 4, 22
  James R., 110
  Samuel, 49, 72, 109
McGinty
  Abednego, 24, 108
  Josiah, 137
  Meashack, 22
  Meshack, 156
  Robert, 24
  Robert, Sr., 156
  William, 156
McGregor
  Alexander, 139
McKean
  John, 43, 66, 110
McKiney
  William, 23
McKinney
  George, 87
  Grissom, 156
  Jane, 23
  Jean, 157
  John, 23, 157
  William, 23, 156
  Wm., 109
McKinnie
  George, 108
McKnight
  James, 137
McLee
  John, 48, 71
McLeod
  Malcom, 137
McMillan
  Daniel, 49, 72
McMullen
  James, 109
McMulling
  James, 24
McMurry
  James, 109

Meacham
  Henry, Jr., 23, 156
  Henry, Sr., 156
  James, 49, 72, 138
Meadows
  Miles, 34, 72
Mecham
  Henry, Sr., 23
Meeks
  Britton, 23, 108
Mercer
  Francis, 23, 108
Mercier
  Benjamin P., 156
Methvin
  Benjamin, 25, 110
  Joseph, 25, 109
  Nathard, 24
Micklejohn
  Robert, 49, 72, 109
Miles
  Aquilla, 157
  John, 22, 156
  Meadows, 34, 49
  Robert P., 22, 111
  Thomas, 22, 109
  William, 89, 138
  William, Jr., 156
Miller
  Bazel, 88
  Ezekiel, 87, 88, 136
  Jacob, 24, 111
  Jesse, 88, 109
  John, 137
  Jonathan, 136
  Nathaniel, 35, 50, 73, 109
  Nathaniel A., 87
  William, 87, 109, 111
Mim, 48, 71
Mimms
  John, 111
Mims
  Gideon, 138
  John, 89, 101
  Needham, 88, 109
  Seaborn, 88

Shadrach, 88
Williamson, 24, 110
Minor
   John B., 50, 73, 137
   Mary, 50, 73, 137
Minter
   Anthony, 87, 110
   James, 88, 138
   John, 138
Mitchel
   D. B., Sr., 24
   Wm. Stephens, 24
Mitchell
   D. B., 108
   John, 49, 50, 72, 73, 138
   Reps, 109
   William S., 156
Mobley
   John, 87
Mobly
   John, 110
Moffit
   Gabriel C., 50, 73
Molpus
   Jeremiah, 50, 73
Moncrief
   Sterling, 49, 72
Montgomery
   James, 50, 73, 137
Moore
   Alfred, 157
   All Can, 156
   Aromenta, 157
   Bartholomew B., 49, 72, 111
   Clement, 24, 110
   Elijah, 25, 110
   Elizabeth, 157
   Ephraim, 50, 73
   Hiram, 111
   James, 138
   Jesse, 137
   John, 157
   John, Jr., 24, 108
   John, Sr., 24, 156
   Levinah, 24, 156
   Luke, 23, 109, 156
   Margaret, 88
   Margarett, 111
   Martha, 157
   Mary, 157
   Morrace, 23
   Morris, 157
   Seabron, 156
   Spencer, 25, 156
   Susan, 157
   Thomas, 88, 111, 137
   Whittington, 24, 156
Moran
   Elisha, 50, 73
   Elizabeth, 139
   Frances, 50, 73, 138
   James, 23, 110
   Jesse, 50, 73, 138
   John, 50, 73, 108
   William, 50, 73, 110
Moreland
   Elisha, 24
Morgan
   Richard M., 48, 71, 110
Morris
   James, 25, 156
   Joseph, 25, 110, 156
   Mary, 137
   Obediah, 50, 73, 110
   Thomas, 111, 156
Moseley
   Joseph, 88
Moses
   Jean, 156
   Margaret, 156
   Martha, 156
   Neal, 137
   Neil, 88
   Saml., 156
Moss
   Epps, 49, 72, 109
   James, 49, 72
Moughon
   Thomas, 24, 157
Munrow
   Daniel, 137
   John, 137

Murden
  Jeremiah, 49, 72, 138
  July, 138
  Mildred, 49, 72
Murphey
  Ellis, 136
Murphy
  Cornelius, 138
  Daniel, 49, 72, 138
  Drury, 49, 72, 108
  Edward M., 138
  Ellis, 49, 72
  James H., 24
Murray
  Jourdan S., 138
Musclewhite
  William, 49, 72
  Wm., 109
Musselwhite
  Redding, 138
Musslewhite
  Drury, 157
  Greene, 157
  Harriet, 157
  Thomas, 157
Myrick
  Goodwin, 24, 111
  James, 23, 110
  John, 23, 108, 109
  Owen, 136
Neeley
  Richard, 51, 74
Newell
  Isaac, 139
Newsom
  Anthony, 51, 74
Newsome
  Anthony, 157
Nichols
  Allen L., 157
Nipper
  William, 51, 74
Norman
  Sherwood, 111
Norris, 4, 10
  Robert, 157

Northcutt
  Robert, 139
O'Daniel
  Alexander, 51, 74, 139
Oates
  James, 25
Ogden
  Solomon, 58, 89, 111
Oler
  John, 139
Oliver
  John, 139
Orme
  Richard M., 51, 74, 111
Owen
  Aaron, 25
Owens
  Aaron, 111
  Anne, 51, 74, 111
  Elijah, 89, 111
  John J., 89, 111
Pace
  David, 52, 75, 111
Page
  James, 158
  Robbin, 158
Paine
  Charles J., 139
Palmer
  Larkin, 158
  Palmer, 158
Palmore
  Christopher, 25
Pardee
  Stephen, 139
Parham
  Benj. J., 158
  Boreland, 25
  Mathew A., 158
  Robert, 158
  Rowland, 113
  Stebb, 24
  Stith, 158
  Thomas, 26
  Thomas S., 112
Parker

Elisha, Jr., 89
George, 25, 112
Henry, 89, 112
Jacob, 25, 112
John, 89, 113
Martha, 89, 139
Polly, 25, 112
Sarah, 25
Simeon, 158
Parr
  James, 51, 74
Parsons
  Josiah, 25
Paschal
  Dennis, 51, 74
Pasmore
  John, 89, 113
Patillo
  Berry, 50, 73
Patton
  William D., 26
Pearman
  Oran D., 112
  Oranj, 26
Pearson
  Abel, 139
Pelham
  Edward, 51, 74
Perdew
  James A., 112
Perdue
  George, 26, 158
  James A., 26, 112
  John D., 26
Perkins
  Leonard, 140
Perry
  Amos P., 158
  James, 158
  Jetson, 139
  Michael W., 89, 112
  Nicholas, 89, 112
  Obed, 89, 112
  Peter, 113
  Solomon, 140
  Willis, 51, 74, 112

Perryman
  John E., 139
  Savility, 139
Persons
  Josiah, 158
Pertilla
  Narcissa, 139
Peters
  John, 26, 112
  Robertson, 112
  Robinson, 26
  Sarah, 26, 112
  William, 26, 112
Petigrew
  James, 89, 112
Petts
  Jack, 26
  John, 26
  Noel, 25
Philips
  Benjamin, 51, 74
Picket
  Betsey, 26
  Elizabeth, 26
  William, 26
Pickett
  Elizabeth, 158
  Richard, 158
  Wm., 158
Pierce
  Lovick, 113
  Lovick, Sr., 51, 74
Pike
  Nathaniel, 51, 74, 112
  Polley, 51, 74
Pine
  Tamsey T., 140
Pitts
  Columbus A., 158
  Henrietta B., 158
  Jack, 158
  Jno., 158
  John, 112
  John D., 140
  Payton T., 158
Pool

Laban, 25, 112
William W., 158
Porter
  Samuel, 51, 74, 112
Porvin
  Joseph, 139
Potee
  Benjamin, 158
  Benjamin P., 158
  Caroline E., 158
  Ellender, 158
  Joseph W., 158
Powell
  James, 89, 113
  Nathan, 46, 69
Preston
  David, 25
Preswood
  Robert, 51, 74, 113
Prichard
  Nathaniel, 112
Pride
  John, 52, 75, 139
Pritchard
  Nathaniel, 86
Proctor
  Martha R., 51, 74
Prosser
  Jesse, 139
Proudfoot
  Hugh W., 139
Pryor
  Marlow, 51, 74, 113
Psalter
  Zabel, 158
Puckett
  John, 140
Pulley
  Benjamin, 52, 75
Pulliam
  William, 51, 74
  Wm., 112
Pully
  Benjamin, 113
Pumphrey
  Reason, 26

Puryear
  William, 140
Quinn
  William, 26, 113
Rabun
  William, 6
Raford
  Patience, 52, 75, 113
Rains
  Allen, 90, 113
Ratclif
  George, 52, 75
Ray
  W. D., 159
  William, 52, 75
Ready
  Isham, 89
  J. Shaw, 145, 159
  John, 89, 140
  Spotswood G., 90
  Spotwood G., 140
  Ursley, 89, 140
Redding
  Archer, 159
  Edith, 27, 114
  Ezekiel, 27
  Haden, 159
  James D., 28
  James F., 159
  James P., 159
  John, 26, 114
  Louiza H., 159
  Malinda, 159
  Martha W., 159
  Parham, 26
  Parham D., 159
  Rowland, 159
  Thomas, 27, 114
  William C., 52, 75, 114
Reed
  Jeremiah, 159
  Zepheniah, 113
  Zephiniah, 27
Reid
  Jane, 27
  Jeremiah, 27

John, 52, 75
Josephus, 140
Templeton, 52, 75, 114
William, 52, 75, 114
Rew
  James, 27
Reynolds
  James, 159
  Joshua, 27, 159
  Mary, 159
  Robert, 159
  Sarah, 27, 159
Rice
  George W., 159
  James, 27, 113, 114
  John, 27, 113
  Nancy, 27, 114
Richards
  Alexander, 140
  Christopher, 75
  Christopher C., 52, 113
Richirson
  Elbert, 27
Riddle
  Willie, 90, 114
  Willis, 113
Rives
  James T., 140
Robertson
  Henry, 27, 114
  John R., 113
  Luke, 145, 159
  William, 52, 75, 113
Robinson
  John R., 53, 76
  Luke, 53, 76, 145, 159
  Simon P., 140
  Solomon, 52, 75
  William, 53, 76, 114
Rockwell
  Samuel, 140
Rodgers
  Cannon R., 113
Rogers
  Cannon R., 89
  George W., 27

  Polly, 159
  William B., 159
Rona
  Joseph, 52, 75
Roper
  John M., 159
Rousseau
  James, 52, 75, 114
  Thomas, 140
Rowe
  Chancey, 34, 52, 114
  Chauncey, 34, 75
Roys
  Mariah, 140
Rucker
  George, 52, 75
  Jane, 52, 75
  Mary Anne, 52, 75
  Willis, 52, 75
Runnels
  James, 28
  Robert, 28
  William, 27
Runnolds
  William, 159
Russel, 125, 145
  James, 27
  John, 27, 114
  Martin, 27, 113
Russell, 4, 10
Rutherford
  Benjamin H., 159
  R., 58
  Robert, 52, 75, 114
  William, 90
  Williams, 140
Rutledge
  Christopher, 14, 114
Ryan
  Rachael, 114
  Risden, 27
  Risdon, 113
Sale
  Gideon, 28, 115
Salter
  Richard, 53, 76, 115

Sanders
  Stephen, 34, 76, 141
Sanford
  Frederick, 53, 76, 140
  Jess, 54, 77
  Jesse, 114
Sarell
  John B., 160
Saunders
  Stephen, 34, 53
Sawyer
  Charles, 160
  Zadock, 160
Scoggin
  James, 28
Scogin
  Smith, Jr., 161
Scott
  John, 91, 116
  John R., 28, 160
  Ross, 28, 115
  Thomas, 91
Scroggin
  William D., 160
Scrogin
  James, 160
Scurlock
  Daniel, 53, 76
  John, 160
  Joshua, 28, 160
Searcy
  Aaron, 29, 160
  Benjamin R., 161
  William, 29, 160
Selby
  Joseph, 56, 79, 115
Sentell
  William, 141
Settle
  Abram, 16
Shackelford
  Edmund, 115
Shackleford
  Edmund, 54, 77
Sharp
  Cyrus, 28, 114

Esley, 141
  John, 90, 116
Sheffield
  Bartley, 91, 115
Shelby
  Evans, 91
Shelly
  Evans, 115
Sheppar
  Charles, 116
Sheppard
  David, 160
  Thomas, 29
  William, 29, 115
Shepperd
  Chas., 28
  David, 28
Shuffield
  Bartley, 115
Shurlock
  Daniel, 115
Simmons
  Elijah, 160
Simons
  John, Sr., 28
Simpson
  George, 54, 77, 160
  James M., 140
  John, 53, 76
  Joseph S., 116
  William, 29
Sims
  Bartlet, 28
  Benjamin, 28, 53, 76
  Benjamin A., 141
  Joseph, 54, 77, 116
  Judith, 29, 161
Skinner
  Ebenezar, 160
  Flora, 28
  Florey, 160
  Henry, 28, 160
  Isaac Alfred, 160
  Jacob, 141
  John, 160
  Larkin, 160

William, 160
Slade
  Joseph L., 74
  Joseph P., 115
  Joseph R., 35
  Joseph T., 51
Slaughter
  Daniel, 54, 77
  Frances, 141
  Frances G., 141
  John, 161
Sledge
  Alexander, 90, 141
Slick
  Joseph, 116
Smallpeace
  Ann, 116
Smallpiece
  Ann, 29
  Thomas Andrew Jackson, 161
  Thomas P., 29
  Thos., 161
Smith
  Charles, 90, 116
  James, 23, 54, 77, 115, 116
  John, 29, 54, 77, 115, 141, 160
  John H., 90, 141
  John R., 54, 77, 141
  Marshal, 20
  Mary, 160
  Samuel T., 28
  Sarah, 54, 58, 77, 115
  William Thomas, 91
Snipes
  Jonathan, 91, 114
  William B., 29
Snow
  Ebenezer, 91, 116
  Salley, 91
  Sarah, 141
  Stephen W., 141
  Synadonia, 141
Sparrow
  James, 141
Spencer
  Alonson, 53, 76

  Richard, 161
Spier
  John M., 160
Spikes
  Andrew, 160
Stackpole
  Thomas, 141
Stanford
  James, 53, 76, 116
Steele
  Elizabeth, 91, 141
  Josh., 40, 63
  Sampson, 91, 141
  William F., 9
Steeley
  James, 54, 77
Steely
  James, 115
Stephens, 4, 33, 93, 125, 163
  Hubert, 114
  Isaac, 90, 141
  John, 90
  Lewis, 4, 90, 141
  Simeon L., 53, 76, 115
  William, 28, 115
Stevens
  John, 29, 115, 160
Stinson
  William, 91, 141
Stone
  Michael, 53, 76, 115
  William D., 54, 77
Stoughtenburg
  Peter B., 53, 76
Stoutenburgh
  Peter B., 141
Stovall
  Joseph, 53, 76, 140
Strickland
  Archibald, 91
Stubbs
  Baradell P., 53, 76, 140
  Peter, 53, 76, 116
  Thomas B., 53, 76, 114
Sturges
  Benja. H., 115

Benjamin H., 53, 76
Daniel, 53, 76, 141
Stutes
  David, 140
Summerton
  Thomas, 54, 77, 115
Swan
  Ebenezer, 53, 76
  Salley, 53, 76
Swillivant
  Elijah, 90, 115
Talbot
  Benjamin, 29, 117
Talbott
  Benjamin, 117
Taliaferro, 4, 33, 54, 77, 93
  Richard C., 55, 78
Tansey
  David, 161
  Eli, 161
Tapley
  Joel, 91, 142
  Watkins, 142
  William, 161
Tarentine
  Samuel, 29, 116
Tarpley
  Jared, 142
Taurence
  Amelius, 90
  Andrew, 90
  Esther, 90
  Mansfield, 90
Taylor
  Bartholomew, 29
  Eden, 90, 142
  Martha, 55, 78
  William, 55, 78, 117
  William D., 90, 117
Terondet
  James C., 54, 77, 142
Terrell
  Barksdale, 94
Terry
  Nathaniel, 90, 116, 117
  Richard, 91, 142

Thomas
  David, 55, 78, 117, 142
  Elizabeth, 162
  Emmaly, 162
  George, 54, 77
  Gracy, 30, 117
  James, 30, 117, 162
  John S., 142
  Jonathan, 30, 162
  Martin, 162
  Mary, 142
  Sherrod, 55, 78
  Spencer, Jr., 30, 117
  Spencer, Sr., 30, 117
Thompkins
  John, 91
Thompson
  Henry, 30, 117
  James, 91, 116, 117
  William, 91, 117
  William H., 162
Thornton
  Henry, 54, 77, 116
Tickner
  Orray, 161
Tiller
  Bagwell B., 161
  Joseph, 161
  Paul Han, 161
Tinsley
  Samuel, 30
  Thomas, 143
Tomkins
  John, 116
Tomlinson
  Benjamin C., 161
  J. D. Maryann, 161
  James, 29, 161
  John, 29, 161
  Mary, 29, 161
  Sarah, 161
Tompkins
  Jane, 55, 78, 142
  John, 117
  William, 142
  Wm., 55, 78

Torrance
  Amilius, 142
  Andrew, 142
  Esther, 142
  Mansfield, 142
  William H., 142
Trapp, 58
  Philip, 142
  Phillip, 54, 77
  Rachel, 142
  Thomas, 54, 77
  Timothy, 91, 116
Trice
  Benjamin, 161
  Elisha, 161
  James Madison, 161
  Jean, 161
  Louiza L. Amanda M., 161
  Martha Ann, 161
  Patience, 161
  Thomas Jefferson, 161
  Willis, 143
Triplet
  Daniel, 87
Triplett
  David, 42, 65
Tripplett
  Daniel, 117
Troutman
  Hiram, 91
  Hiram B., 142
  Isaac N., 142
  John, 91, 116
Tucker
  Joseph, 54, 77, 116
  Samuel, 142
Tulley
  John A., 54, 77
Tully
  John A., 117
Turk
  Thomas, 90, 117
Turner
  Asa A., 162
  Elisha, 142
  Henry, 90, 117

  Joseph, 142
  Joshua, 54, 77, 116, 117
  Milborn, 55, 78
  Shelburn, 117
  Wilson, 30
Underwood
  Enoch, 92, 117
Varner
  Alexander, 118
  Alexandria, 30
Vass
  John M., 55, 78, 118
Veazey
  James, 30, 162
  Thomas, 30, 162
Vickers
  Hatcher, 118
  Nancy, 55, 78, 143
  V. E., 4
  Vincent E., 55, 78, 143
Vincent
  Benjamin, 30, 118
Virdin
  Elizabeyh, 143
  Jane, 143
Walker
  Barshaba, 163
  Baurshayba, 32
  Eli, 30
Wall
  Eliza, 55, 78
  Elizabeth, 144
  James, 144
Wallace
  Enoch, 91, 118
Waller
  Elizabeth, 30
Wallis
  John, 144
Waltern
  Henry W., 31
Walters
  John C., 144
Walton
  Henry W., 162
Ware

John H., 55, 78, 143
William W., 56, 79
Warren
  Robert, 31, 120
Washburn
  Joseph, 144
Washington
  Robert B., 55, 78, 118, 120
  Robert B., Jr., 55, 78
Watson, 10
  Alexander, 31, 118
  Alexander, Jr., 56, 79, 118
  Allen, 56, 79, 143
  Caty, 55, 78
  James C., 31, 118, 119
  John, 31, 32, 162
  John, Sr., 31, 162
  Robert, 31, 55, 78, 144
  Robert T., 163
  Samuel, 31, 119
  William C., 31, 118
Weatherly
  Louiza, 143
  William, 55, 78
Weeker
  Robert, 82
Weeks
  William, 55, 78, 119
Welch
  Welch, 80
  William, 57, 119
Whallis
  Francis, 56, 79, 119
Wheeler
  David, 57, 80, 120
  Francis A. B., 163
  Henry, 162
  Jesse, 119
Wheler
  Asberry, 31
  Henry, 31
  Jesse, 31
Whitaker
  Mark, 92, 120
  Simon, 56, 79, 120
White, 4, 125, 163

Beersheba, 92
Benadick, 30
Benedict, 118, 119
Benjamin, 4
  George, 144
  John, 92
  John E., 143
  Rachel, 92, 143
  William, 92, 143
Whitfield
  Allums, 162
Whitney
  Elisha, 144
Whittle
  Ambrose, 144
Wicker
  Charlotte, 144
  John, 92, 118
  John A., 144
  Wiley, 144
Wickers
  Julius, 12, 144
Wiggins, 4
Wiley
  Ann, 162
  J. Eliza, 162
  John B., 162
  Lard H., 162
  Leroy M., 144
  Moses, 56, 79, 162
  Sarah Ann, 162
Wilkerson
  Malcomb G., 92
  Nancy, 93, 120
  Sherod, 93
Wilkinson
  Drury, 143
  Malcom G., 120
  Sherod, 119
Willey
  Leroy M., 55, 78
Williams, 131
  Anderson, 55, 78, 118
  John, 55, 78, 92, 120
  Mary, 92, 120
  Thomas, 92, 120

William, 32
Winfrey, 32, 119
Williamson
　Charles, 56, 79, 88, 119
　Eugene, 56
　Eugene J., 79, 118
　Randol, 92
Willingham
　Charles, 119
　James, 31, 119
Willis
　Britton, 93, 143
　Keziah, 93
　Kissiah, 143
　Price, 93, 120
　Robert, 92, 93, 143
　Robert, Jr., 143
　William, 56, 79, 118
　Williamson, 92, 119
Willowby
　John, 57, 80
Wilson
　Elizabeth, 163
　James, 56, 79, 120
　Lemuel, 86, 119
　William, 144
Winaham
　John, 30
Windham
　John, 119, 120
Wingate
　Amos, 144
　Emanuel, 144
　Michael, 119
Winget
　Amos, 56, 79
　Emmanuel, 57, 80
　Michael, 56, 79
　Richard B., 56, 79
Winn
　Baylor, 31
Wise
　John, 143
Wiseman
　John, 56, 79
Wittingham

Charles M., 31
Womack
　Green, 31
　Mark, 32, 120
Womble
　Drury, 22, 162
　Edmund, 163
　Mariah, 162
Wommack
　Green, 118
Wood
　Elisha, 56, 79, 120, 124
　Hiram A., 143
　John, 26, 118
Woodall
　Archibald, 56, 79, 120
　Jacob, 31, 162
　Tempy, 162
Woodbrooks
　William, 31
Woodward, 4
Woolsey
　Benjamin, 93, 119
Wootan
　John, 143
Wooten
　John, 56, 79
Wooton
　John, 93
Works
　Eli, 30, 119
Worsham
　Archer, Jr., 91, 118, 119
　Archer, Sr., 92, 118
　Daniel B., 92, 119
　David, 92, 143
　David G., 92, 143
　George S., 30, 144
　Jeremiah, 56, 79, 144
　John G., 92, 144
　Patrick H., 92
Wright
　Abednego, 118
　Abednigo, Sr., 31
　Charlton, 56, 79, 144
　John H., 56, 79, 118

Pryor, 56, 79, 144
  William, 56, 79
Wynn
  Anderson Westmoreland, 162
  Charles R., 162
  Gabriel, 162
  John Westley, 162
  Patsey, 162
  Robert, 10, 162
  Robert Tarpley, 162
  Sarah Hobbs, 162
  Shady Ann Mason, 162
  Thomas Harrison, 162
Yarborough
  Benjamin, 120
Yates
  Willis, 120
Yats
  Willis, 32
Yeargam
  Benjamin H., 32
Young
  Amos, 93, 120, 125, 163
  Marmaduke N., 163
  Thomas, 32, 120
  Turner, 32, 120
Youngblood
  Thomas, 32

www.ingramcontent.com/pod-product-compliance
Lightning Source LLC
Chambersburg PA
CBHW070249230426
43664CB00014B/2465